THE GPS
HANDBOOK

THE GPS HANDBOOK

Revised and Updated Edition

Robert I. Egbert
and Joseph E. King

Burford Books

Printed in the United States of America.

10   9   8   7   6   5   4   3   2   1

Library of Congress Cataloging-in-Publication Data
        Egbert, Robert I.
        The GPS handbook : an outdoorsman's guide /
        Robert I. Egbert and Joseph E. King.
                p.   cm.
        Includes bibliographical references and index.
        ISBN 978-1-58080-149-2 (pbk.)
        1. Outdoor recreation—Equipment and supplies.   2. Global
Positioning System.   3. Orienteering—Equipment and
supplies.   4. Navigation—Equipment and supplies.   I. Title:
Global Positioning System handbook.   II. King, Joseph E.,
1947–   III. Title.

GV191.623.E43   2003
910'.285—dc21
2003004959

Contents

Introduction to the Revised Edition

Science and technology continue to advance at an ever increasing pace. This is particularly true in the world of Global Positioning Systems (GPS). For the outdoorsman, these advances in GPS have made it much easier to accurately navigate while in the field. In the first edition of this book, many of the GPS units that had sufficient memory capacity to store digital maps, were also rather large, bulky, and typically consumed power at a rate that rapidly drained batteries. Such units, while suitable for use the automobiles, were poor choices for carrying in the field. Now, a number of small, compact, GPS units with maps stored in their memories are available. Such units are easily carried afield and yet have minimal power consumption.

This has all changed in the few short years since the first edition of *The GPS Handbook* was published. These advances in GPS units, as well as some overall improvements and changes in GPS in general, suggested that it was time for the authors to update the book.

This second edition generally follows the outline of the original book. However, each chapter has been revised to reflect new information, correct errors in the first edition, or to further clarify or expand certain topics that have become more important. Chapter 2 entitled, Equipment Options has been extensively rewritten to reflect the newer GPS units now on the market. As in the first edition, our focus has continued to be on terrestrial (land-based) GPS units that are suitable for carrying while enjoying one or more of the many forms of outdoor recreation (hiking, climbing, biking, hunting, etc.).

The authors wish to thank the number of readers who have contacted us with questions, comments, or suggestions about the book. We also would like to thank the various GPS manufacturers for providing us with valuable technical details about their products. Finally, we would like to express our appreciation to Peter Burford, of Burford Books, Inc., who has now guided us through two editions of *The GPS Handbook*.

 # Preface

Whether looking for your deer stand in the dark, trying to find your cousin's duck blind in strange country, or walking out of a wilderness in the fog, land navigation is a handy skill for anyone who spends time outdoors. Getting lost, or not getting where you want to go in an expeditious manner, may merely cause inconvenience, embarrassment, or less time afield, but on occasion it can mean disaster. Each year, in the United States alone, hundreds of people get lost while involved in some outdoor activity and have to be rescued by search teams. Many others miss out on some outdoor opportunities altogether or lose valuable time because they are unable to locate a particular campsite, trailhead, hunting spot, or fishing hole. Modern, easy-to-use Global Positioning System (GPS) receivers, available for as little as $100, have made finding your way in the great outdoors an easy task.

This is the same technology in which the U.S. military has placed complete confidence. Celestial navigation, for centuries the key to navigation for mariners around the world, is no longer preeminent at the U.S. Naval Academy; instead the focus is on GPS. GPS provides satellite signals that can be analyzed by a GPS receiver to compute position, velocity, and time. This book is about how to select and effectively use a GPS receiver to make your time outdoors safer, easier, and more fun.

Note that GPS has many other applications that include such diverse activities as tracking trucks and other vehicles, land surveying, and accurate bomb delivery. This book specifically focuses on outdoor terrestrial (land-based) recreational GPS use. There are so many unique marine applications of GPS that the topic would have to be treated in a separate book.

We assume no previous knowledge of GPS in this text; beginners will find all they need to get started. Experienced GPS users, however, will also find this book useful.

Chapter 1 gives a general description of the Global Positioning System and how it works. The next chapter discusses the various makes and models of GPS receivers currently available. Since using a GPS receiver effectively requires a basic understanding of map reading and land navigation, these topics are covered in chapters 3 and 4. From there, chapters 5 through 7 cover various aspects of using GPS in the outdoors. A fairly new but important development in GPS technology is the ability to interface a GPS receiver with a personal computer. Chapter 8 discusses some of the software programs commercially available to assist in this process. The remaining chapters discuss a variety of issues raised by and related to GPS. Finally, a list of books about GPS and some GPS Web sites are included in the appendices.

CHAPTER 1

An Introduction to GPS

In order to make the best use of a GPS, it is important to have at least a basic understanding of the way it works. This chapter gives an overview of the Global Positioning System, describes how it operates, and explains how it can be used to determine a precise location anywhere on earth.

The idea of a Global Positioning System or GPS was conceived in the 1970s by the U.S. Department of Defense (DoD). The original motivation behind the development of the system was the need for ballistic missile submarines to accurately determine their position before launching missiles. The other positioning systems available at that time were limited in range, too complicated, affected by atmospheric conditions, or subject to jamming and interference.

The backbone of the GPS system is a constellation of 24 NAVSTAR satellites located in precise orbits, each approximately 10,900 miles above the earth. These satellites were launched by the DoD at a cost of $12 billion. Each satellite weights about 4,000 pounds and is approximately 17 feet long with its solar panels extended. The satellites orbit the earth every 12 hours. They have an estimated life of seven and a half years each, but the system will be maintained, and new replacement satellites are planned.

In addition to the 24 GPS satellites, five ground stations monitor the satellites to make sure that they operate correctly and maintain their exact position in space. The ground stations are located in Hawaii, Ascension Island, Diego Garcia, Kwajalein, and Colorado Springs.

Each GPS satellite contains a high-frequency radio transmitter that sends information back to earth. A GPS receiver locks on to these signals, and by a process known as triangulation—which will be discussed in more detail shortly—can accurately determine its location anywhere on earth. GPS operates 24 hours a day and in all weather conditions. This allows GPS to be used for precise navigation on land, on water, and in the air.

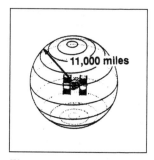

We are somewhere on this sphere.

TRIANGULATION

The concepts behind the operation of the GPS are relatively simple, although the electronics required are quite sophisticated. Basically, a GPS receiver determines position by calculating the distance to three or more of the GPS satellites by a process loosely referred to as *triangulation*.

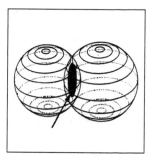

A second satellite narrows down our location.

For example, let's assume that we find ourselves at a point in space 11,000 miles from a particular GPS satellite. This would mean that we could be located at any point on the surface of a sphere with a radius of 11,000 miles that is centered on the particular GPS satellite (see illustration). Next, suppose that we determine the distance from our

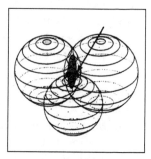

A third satellite puts us at either of two points. Courtesy Timble.

(as-yet-unknown) location to a second GPS satellite and find that this distance is 12,000 miles. This implies that we are also located on the surface of a second sphere with a radius of 12,000 miles centered on the second satellite. Now we can see that we must be located somewhere on the circle that is defined by where the two spheres intersect. If we calculate the distance between our location and a third satellite and find that this distance is, say, 13,000 miles, then using the same logic as before we find that we must be located on either one of the two points defined by the intersection of the three spheres. Usually one of these two points can be eliminated as a possible location because it is unrealistically far from the earth, or for other reasons. However, we can determine our true location without any guesswork by measuring the distance to a fourth GPS satellite. As we will see later, there is also another advantage in using a fourth measurement.

MEASURING DISTANCE

All this may seem well and good—but how do we determine the (generally large) distances between our unknown location and the GPS satellites? Rather than measuring these distances directly, which would be a challenge, a GPS receiver measures the time it takes for the radio signal transmitted from each satellite to reach the location of the receiver. Since radio waves travel at the speed of light, which is roughly 186,000 miles per second, by measuring the time it takes for the signal from each satellite to travel to the receiver, the distance from the receiver to the satellite can be calculated by multiplying the travel time by the speed of the radio waves. We use the same process when we determine that an automobile traveling at 50 miles per hour for 3 hours travels 150 miles (50 miles/hour × 3 hours = 150 miles).

PRECISE TIME MEASUREMENT

At this point, it may seem that we have just traded one difficult problem for another. While measuring the distance from an unknown point to a satellite in space may seem complex, determining the time it takes for a signal traveling at 186,000 miles per second to cross that distance is obviously going to require a very accurate stopwatch. Even if the satellite is 15,000 miles from the GPS receiver, it will take only a little more than 0.08 seconds for the signal to reach the receiver.

Time measurement this accurate is accomplished by having each satellite generate its own unique signal, which is also stored in the GPS receiver. The receiver essentially compares the internal signal with the one received from the satellite—which of course is delayed, since it has had to travel some 11,000 miles or more to reach the receiver. The time difference between a certain signal value in the internal signal and the same value in the delayed satellite signal is equal to the travel time. If we multiply this time difference by the speed of the radio wave, we obtain the distance.

However, we must still be sure that the clocks in both the satellites and the GPS receivers are precisely synchronized, since small differences in the time kept by these two clocks could represent hundreds of miles of error in the calculated distances. To ensure accurate timekeeping in the GPS satellites, each one is equipped with an atomic clock, which actually uses the oscillation frequency of a particular atom as a time reference. Atomic clocks are the most accurate timekeeping mechanism known to humanity.

Unfortunately atomic clocks are quite costly, and installing them in GPS receivers would make these receivers so expensive that they would be impractical. Few people would be able to afford them.

Instead, the GPS developers came up with a clever trick that allows the use of much less accurate (and also much less expensive) clocks in GPS receivers. The trick involves measuring the distance from an unknown point to a fourth satellite. Remember, three measurements would be enough if we could eliminate one of the two possible locations resulting from three satellite measurements.

If the clock in the GPS receiver kept perfect time and was perfectly synchronized with those in the GPS satellites, then it would be possible to determine an unknown location with only three measurements, assuming that we could logically eliminate the second possible location point. Since in reality the clock in the GPS receiver is imperfect, however, a fourth measurement will indicate a discrepancy between the location predicted by the first three measurements and that predicted by the fourth. The GPS receiver is programmed to recognize that this discrepancy is due to imperfect timekeeping. Since the time offset in the GPS receiver affects all the measurements, the receiver is programmed to look for a correction factor that it can subtract from all four timing measurements so that the predicted locations from all of them lie at single point. By continually repeating this process, the GPS receiver is able to maintain the accurate time needed to determine a specific location. The consequence of this timing-correction trick is that a GPS receiver will need to have at least four channels so that it can pick up the signals from the four satellites it needs to make accurate, time-corrected measurements.

SATELLITE POSITIONS

In all the discussion above, we have assumed that the exact locations of the GPS satellites are known so that we can use them as reference points. It turns out, however, that perfect satellite orbits—like perfect timekeeping—are not possible in the real world. Fortunately, things are not as bad as they seem. First of all, the GPS satellites are placed in orbit some 11,000 miles above the surface of the earth. This is a relatively high altitude, and as a result the GPS satellites are free from any interference by the earth's atmosphere. This means that their positions in orbit can be accurately predicted using relatively simple mathematics.

In addition, all 24 of the GPS satellites were launched into very precise orbits and spaced around the earth in such a way that signals from at least five of them can be picked up at any point on the globe. The last of the 24 GPS satellites was launched in March 1994. Four additional GPS satellites have been kept in reserve and can be launched to replace any satellites that should fail for some unexpected reason. All GPS receivers have the exact, moment-by-moment location of each GPS satellite stored in their memory.

Besides inserting the GPS satellites into precise orbits, the Department of Defense continually tracks these satellites with very precise radar. The radar detects any minor variation in the satellite orbits caused by the gravitational pull of the sun or moon as well as any other factor. The errors in position are transmitted back up to the satellites; each one then includes this revised position information in the timing signals it broadcasts.

OTHER SOURCES OF ERROR

By now it must seem like we've eliminated all the difficulties associated with GPS. As might be expected, though, there are still a few problems. One of these involves our initial assumption that the speed of light is constant. While it is true that the speed of light is constant in a vacuum, as the GPS signal from an orbiting satellite travels to the earth it passes through charged particles in the ionosphere (the outer portion of the earth's atmosphere) and water vapor in the troposphere (the inner portion of the atmosphere). The signal slows down as it passes through both of these atmospheric layers. The result is an error similar to that caused by bad clocks. Furthermore, once the GPS signal gets to the earth, it can bounce off tall buildings and other obstructions before getting to the receiver. This is called *multipath error*. Finally, the GPS receiver can pick up noise—signals besides the one from the GPS satellite. All of the above factors can degrade GPS accuracy. There are techniques available to mitigate the effects of these error sources, and most GPS receivers employ several of them. The exact details of such techniques are beyond the scope of this book.

GPS ACCURACY

A summary of the effects of each of the various error sources on GPS accuracy is given in table 1. It should be emphasized that the error values listed in the table are in feet and are typical values per each satellite. The errors due to each source are not necessarily cumulative, however; it would thus be incorrect to simply add up the individual error figures for each source to determine a typical range of GPS accuracy with all error sources acting simultaneously.

TABLE 1. Summary of GPS Error Sources

Source	Typical Error (In Feet)
Satellite clocks	5.0
Orbit errors	8.2
Ionosphere	16.4
Troposphere	1.6
Receiver noise	1.0
Multipath errors	2.0

DIFFERENTIAL GPS

Differential GPS (DGPS) is a way to provide even more accurate position information. A DGPS system requires the use of two GPS receivers. One of these receivers is placed at a spot that has already been precisely determined—we know exactly where it is located. The second GPS receiver is then allowed to move around normally. These two receivers are generally located relatively close to each other when compared to the distances to the GPS satellites, so both receivers pick up the same signals. However, since the stationary GPS receiver knows its location precisely, it can use the information it receives to determine the timing errors coming from the satellite signals. The stationary GPS receiver then transmits the timing-error-correction information to the moving receiver, which enables it to make much more accurate position determinations.

Using DGPS, the errors from satellite clocks and orbit ir-regularities can be eliminated, and errors that occur as the satellite signals pass through the atmosphere can be signif-icantly minimized. Unfortunately, receiver noise errors and multipath errors are still present because they are either unique to the receiver (receiver errors) or occur right at the receiver (multipath errors).

We mention DGPS because those interested in GPS tech-nology are quite likely to hear this term. However, we believe that DGPS will be of little practical use for outdoor recre-ation. The added cost of the stationary receiver and the need for a precise location to install it will make DGPS unattractive for most outdoors people. Also, the improvements in accu-racy achieved by DGPS are probably overkill for most recre-ational activities. DGPS's most significant applications are in fields such as surveying, oil and gas exploration, and map-ping, where more accurate measurements are crucial.

WIDE AREA AUGMENTATION SYSTEM

The Wide Area Augmentation System (WAAS) is a GPS en-hancement that has significantly improved accuracy with-out the need for an additional DGPS receiver. A system of two geostationary satellites (not the regular GPS satellites) and about 25 ground stations provides signal correction that results in accuracy of 3 meters or less 95 percent of the time. At present this is available only in North America, but the service will likely be available across much of the globe within a few years. At present there are no ground reference stations in South America. GPS users in South America can receive the WAAS signal, but the signal is not corrected and so does not improve the accuracy of the GPS unit. In Asia, the Japanese are developing the Multi-Function Satellite Aug-mentation System (MSAS). The Europeans are working on the Euro Geostationary Navigation Overlay Service (EGNOS). In time, GPS worldwide will have access to improved accu-racy through these and other similar systems still to come.

If you are shopping for a new GPS receiver, make sure it is "WAAS capable" if you desire the greatest precision at the lowest cost.

SELECTIVE AVAILABILITY

Although GPS was originally developed for military use, the U.S. government quickly realized that there were numerous civilian applications for the system. As a result, the Department of Defense created two different GPS satellite transmission codes. One code was designated the P code (for "precision") and was for military use. The second was known as the C/A (for "civilian access") code and was, of course, intended for civilian use. Once the system was up and running, however, it was found that civilian GPS receivers using the C/A code were more accurate than the DoD had anticipated. As a result, the military developed a system for degrading the GPS signals sent to civilian GPS receivers. This intentional degradation in GPS accuracy is known as *selective availability* or *S/A*. S/A reduced civilian GPS accuracy to within 300 feet or less about 95 percent of the time. Typical accuracy, however, for most users was between 60 and 160 feet.

It is important to note that as of May 2, 2000, *selective availability has been deactivated.* Instead, the Department of Defense has now developed the ability to keep GPS signals from reaching certain selected areas. However, GPS remains subject to the U.S. national command authorities (as do all other navigation programs provided by the federal government). As such, S/A could be reactivated if deemed necessary for security purposes, although the U.S. government has indicated that it has no intention of doing so either now or in the future.

CHAPTER 2

➤ Equipment Options

Now that we've obtained a little background about GPS and how it works, it's time to look at the different GPS receivers on the market today. If you're new to GPS, your first look at all the receivers available, with their unique features, may be a bit overwhelming. Don't worry! We'll take this one step at a time, starting with the basic units and their features and working up to the more advanced receivers.

GPS receivers can be divided into the following categories:

1. Basic GPS receivers without map display capability.
2. GPS receivers with map display capability—the most common outdoors-oriented GPS.
3. GPS receivers integral to personal digital assistants (PDAs), Pocket PCs, and multimedia cell phones.
4. GPS receivers linked or integral to laptop computers.

The GPS receivers currently available in each of the above categories, along with a summary of their features, are listed in a table at the end of this chapter.

TERMINOLOGY

Before proceeding with descriptions of the GPS receivers commonly used for outdoor navigation, we need to define a few more terms that will help clarify the different features contained in the various models.

Channels

In chapter 1, as you may recall, we described how we could accurately determine our position by triangulating the signals from four different GPS satellites. To do this, the GPS receiver must of course be capable of receiving signals from at least four different GPS satellites. Receivers thus employ what are commonly known as *channels*. A channel in a GPS receiver is capable of receiving and processing the signal from a single GPS satellite. A single-channel GPS receiver works by sequentially tuning through the signals from the different GPS satellites that are in range. The receiver monitors the signal from one particular satellite for a few milliseconds, stores the information, then proceeds to monitor the signal from the next satellite and store it before moving on to another satellite. While this process works, it does take some time. Thus it will take a bit longer for a single-channel receiver lock on to the available GPS satellites. In addition, if you are moving, you may pass by trees or other structures that temporarily block the signal from a particular GPS satellite. If that satellite happens to be the one your single-channel GPS receiver is attempting to monitor, the accuracy of the position determination may be degraded somewhat.

Virtually all GPS receivers today, including the basic models, have at least 12-channel capability. While this may seem like a bit of overkill, in actuality the 12-channel capacity allows the receiver to "select" the signals from all the different satellites that are in range. Since the four or more satellite signals needed are received and processed simultaneously, a multichannel receiver operates slightly faster than a single-channel unit. In addition, if you happen to be moving and cross some obstacle that temporarily blocks the signal from one or more satellites, the multichannel receiver quickly selects a different satellite to complete the position calculation.

Since in any location it is rare to be able to pick up the signals from more than 10 GPS satellites, the typical 12-channel capability of today's GPS receivers is probably the maximum that will ever be needed, although some new units have 16 or even 20-channel capability. Due to the remarkable capabilities of modern integrated electronic circuit manufacturing, the incremental cost of producing a multichannel GPS receiver over a single-channel unit with a sequential processor is quite small.

Waypoints/Landmarks

Waypoint and *landmark* are the GPS names for the coordinates of a specific location. GPS receivers require that a waypoint not only contain the coordinate values of a location but also be assigned a simple name, such as *camp, tower, dock,* or the like. Waypoints are key elements in GPS navigation. To get to a specific location, for example, you would enter the waypoint for that particular spot into the memory of the GPS receiver. The receiver would then determine your present position and calculate the direction and distance from your present location to your desired destination.

Some GPS receivers have more memory than others and as a result are able to store a larger number of waypoints. This can be useful, since longer trips can require more waypoints. Most GPS receivers today can store at least 250 waypoints; many are capable of storing 500 to 1,000 waypoints.

Routes/Tracks

A *route is* a set of waypoints that define the path you intend to travel. A *track* is a collection of points that show the path you have actually traveled. A *track log is* the collection of these points as stored in the memory of a GPS receiver. As before, GPS receivers with more memory can store a greater number of routes and record longer track logs. Each portion of a route between two adjacent waypoints is called a *leg*.

INITIALIZING YOUR NEW GPS RECEIVER

Every GPS contains an almanac of data describing the constellation of GPS satellites. However, the receiver may need a bit of help "finding itself" the first time it is used, if it has been moved a considerable distance since last used—say, 300 miles or more—or if its memory has been fully erased. This process is typically referred to as *initialization*.

The specific details of the initialization procedure depend on the GPS receiver manufacturer. In some cases, different receiver models from the same manufacturer may have different initialization procedures.

For example, the Garmin eTrex Legend, a common GPS receiver, has a "New Location" feature whereby the user uses the eTrex "click stick" to scroll down an options menu to "New Location" and is prompted to a map which can be panned across to specify the approximate new location of the receiver. This process makes locating the receiver by GPS satellites much quicker.

At this point, the GPS receiver will begin searching for satellites and should compute your position within two to three minutes at most—often much more quickly. Note that once the receiver has determined your location, it will determine your elevation (or correct your elevation estimate) and correct your approximate time entry to give the precise time.

CREATING A WAYPOINT/LANDMARK

Just as different GPS receivers have different initialization procedures, the procedures for setting waypoints or landmarks will vary. Recall that a *waypoint* or *landmark* is the coordinate of a specific location that is stored in the memory of the GPS receiver. In addition to the coordinate values, the GPS receiver also stores a simple name for the waypoint. Most GPS receivers will automatically generate a name for each landmark, or allow users to create their own names. The number of letters allowed for a user-selected waypoint name depends on the amount of memory available in the GPS receiver. Often this is limited to six to eight characters, although more sophisticated receivers with a lot of memory allow longer names and even a short description of the location.

The eTrex Legend mentioned previously has a multi-functional "Click Stick" button. Pressing this button will create a landmark at the current location. The receiver-generated landmark number will then appear across the display screen along with a prompt that asks you to either accept this name or enter a name of your own. Once the name is selected, you simply highlight "OK" on the screen and press the Click Stick.

To create a waypoint at a position other than your present location with the eTrex, you can either find the new location on the pre-loaded map and highlight a "Save as Waypoint" feature, or you can access the Mark Waypoint page and, after highlighting the Location field at the bottom of the screen, manually enter new lat/lon coordinates.

In any case the newly created landmark is now stored in the memory of the eTrex. The procedures for other GPS receivers are similar.

CREATING ROUTES/TRACKS

The process of creating a route will again vary depending of the specific GPS receiver being used. In the eTrex GPS receiver, routes are created by going to the "Routes" page on the main menu, highlighting "New," pressing the enter button on a blank line to access the "Find" menu, and selecting from the subsequent list of waypoints, cities, and other landmarks. This process is repeated until your route is complete. The eTrex will allow a route to contain up to 50 waypoints. GPS receivers with larger memories will generally allow multiple routes to be stored and also allow more legs per each route.

OTHER CONSIDERATIONS

In addition to initializing your GPS receiver and learning how to create waypoints, routes, and so on, you will also have the opportunity to select the units and format in which your GPS receiver will display information. For example, you can have the time displayed in a 12- or 24-hour format, and also select whether you wish the time displayed to be local time or Greenwich Mean Time (GMT). You can also choose to have your position displayed in longitude/latitude coordinates, Universal Transverse Mercator (UTM) coordinates, or one of several other coordinate options. We'll discuss these different coordinate systems in the next chapter. Fortunately, most GPS receivers are preset to give local time, and to list position in longitude and latitude. After you've gained a little experience with your receiver, you may wish to select some of the other display options.

With this additional bit of background, let's now take a look at some of the GPS units available today.

BASIC GPS RECEIVERS

As the name implies, basic GPS receivers are the simplest and least expensive units on the market today. Often selling for about $100 or less, basic GPS receivers are just as accurate as the more advanced models but do not include some of the extra features incorporated in the more sophisticated receivers. They represent an excellent choice for the GPS beginner or the budget-conscious GPS user. A typical basic unit provides:

Garmin's basic eTrex is an inexpensive 12-channel GPS receiver, but lacks mapping capability. Courtesy: Garmin

➤ Satellite location and signal strength. (This is useful if you are having trouble getting a position fix as a result of overhead shielding—it tells you what portion of the sky to try to get clear.)

➤ Location, typically in the grid of your choice, and estimated position error or EPE.

- Elevation above sea level, although accuracy is typically not all that good.
- Accurate time.
- The ability to record your movement as a set of way-points connected to form tracks and determine the distance traveled.
- The ability to reverse the recorded track and get compass headings for each leg.
- The ability to enter tracks manually and by download from a computer.
- The ability to output a signal to a PDA or notebook computer providing a location signal that can be displayed on a compatible map.

The one useful feature they lack is map display.

GPS RECEIVERS WITH MAP DISPLAY CAPABILITY

The relatively small number of basic GPS receivers on the market today is an indication of the advances in modern integrated electronics. The cost of adding map display capability to the basic GPS unit has become low enough that most makers are including them in even their lower-cost models. Typically there is a base-map, which includes major roadways, towns, and navigational aids on water. If you select a GPS unit with more memory or with optional memory cards you can purchase enhanced maps on CD or by internet download. Depending on the map you select, you can obtain detailed topo maps and even satellite-image overlays. Most of the even moderately-expensive GPS receivers feature bright, full-color screens, which adds much to the ability to see the maps and to the user-friendliness of the unit in general.

GPS RECEIVERS INTEGRATED WITH PERSONAL DIGITAL ASSISTANTS

Personal digital assistants or PDAs started as small electronic "notepads" but have quickly developed into powerful

Garmin eTrex Legend, with mapping capability. Courtesy: Garmin

Delorme's Earthmate PN-20. Courtesy: Delorme

Garmin Colorado 300. Courtesy: Garmin

handheld computerlike devices. Palm, Handspring, and Sony offer PDAs using the Palm operating system (OS). Compaq, Casio, HP (discontinued following the merger with Compaq), and others now offer PDAs running the Windows Pocket PC operating system. Many new PDAs incorporate cell phone capability.

PDAs can be integrated with GPS systems in two ways. Many stand-alone GPS receivers can be interconnected with a PDA via a USB or serial data cable. Using the NMEA inter-face protocol, the physically separate GPS unit sends infor-mation to software running on the PDA, providing location and other information. The advantage of this approach is that when you reach the trail-head, the energy-hungry PDA can be left behind and the lighter, more energy-efficient GPS receiver can be carried with you on the trail. As an alterna-tive, many PDAs incorporate a Compact Flash (CF) memory expansion slot, creating an opportunity to incorporate a GPS receiver as an integral component. Reviews of such systems

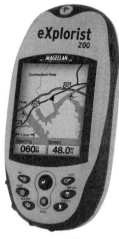

Lowrance iFinder
Expedition.
Courtesy: Lowrance

Magellan Explorist 200.
Courtesy: Magellan

Magellan Triton
1500. Courtesy:
Magellan

have been mixed at best, although failure to use auxiliary antennae may have been a major factor in the disappointing results the some users experienced.

Both approaches allow the GPS receiver to be integrated with useful map or even geographic information system (GIS) software and larger map files than a PDA can handle. PDAs also have a typical screen size of 2.5 by 3 inches, versus 1.4 by 1.4 (on up to 1.6 by 2.0 inches) for a typical GPS receiver. This is particularly useful when traveling in a vehicle since the larger PDA display is much easier to see while driving. Software from companies like NAVMAN and TravRoute not only provides detailed maps, but can also provide detailed navigation guidance—including specific voice commands—telling you when to turn to follow a specified route or to reach a specific destination.

That said, bear in mind that the focus of GPS/PDA interconnections is for street and highway navigation, as opposed to outdoor navigation. We believe it pays to be skeptical about combined PDA/GPS units, which tend to be something like an electronic version of the "Swiss Army Knife." Usually combining too many "gadgets" into one unit results in a compromise, and it is likely that either the GPS or PDA portions of the device, or both, are of less quality than a stand alone version.

GPS RECEIVERS LINKED TO NOTEBOOK COMPUTERS

GPS receivers with serial or USB output capability can also easily be linked to a notebook computer. Notebooks now replicate desktop computer performance and provide access to a wide range of mapping and GPS software. Notebooks, however, require even more energy than a PDA; for a road trip of more than a few hours you'll need a 12-volt DC adapter or an AC inverter to plug the computer into your vehicle's electrical system. The size of a notebook is also an issue. The large screen is great, but handling it can be a serious safety hazard while driving. They work best when mounted in a rack—or better yet, in a passenger's lap. Even more than with PDAs, it is not practical to carry a notebook computer on the trail, unless you have very unusual requirements.

GPS RECEIVERS INTEGRATED WITH CELL PHONES

The Public Safety Act of 1999 (911 Act) directed the Federal Communications Commission (FCC) to "designate 9-1-1 as the universal emergency telephone number within the United States for reporting an emergency to appropriate authorities and requesting assistance." The FCC has issued an order requiring cellular phone service providers to make available enhanced 911 service (E911), which permits emergency operators to locate cell phone distress calls. The first phase required carriers to begin selling and activating handsets with automatic location identification (ALI) by October 1, 2001. It didn't happen. The regulators were ahead of the technology. Additional rules for E911 were announced in spring 2002, requiring that operators be able to pinpoint emergency callers within 300 yards of their location, either through network-based technology that triangulates the user's location through proximity to cell towers, or through handset systems using a GPS transmitter. The FCC's new deadline for nationwide wireless location implementation to begin was December 31, 2005. Cell phones are being completely redesigned so that integral GPS circuitry can share as many parts of the phone as possible. Industry analysts indicate that the cost of adding GPS capability to a cell phone may eventually fall as low as $10. Keep in mind that for a typical cell phone, this will be an emergency location feature, not a robust navigation system. Many "Smartphones" incorporate GPS road-navigation systems, similar to those available in PDA's but, like the PDA-based systems, they are intended primarily for use in automobiles and are inadequate for off-road outdoors navigation.

GPS RECEIVERS WITH SENSORS

A GPS receiver is an excellent compass—as long as you are moving. When you stop, the lack of motion prevents the unit from calculating direction. Garmin's GPSMAP 76S and other units incorporate digital compasses, which provide direction bearings while standing still. These units also incorporate a barometric altimeter to offer more accurate elevation readings.

The Garmin's specifications include:

➤ **An electronic compass** accurate to within 2 degrees with proper calibration (typical) or 5 degrees in extreme northern and southern latitudes, and resolution to 1 degree.

➤ **A barometric altimeter** accurate to within 10 feet with proper calibration (user and/or automatic calibration), and resolution to 1 foot. Its range is −2,000 to 30,000 feet.

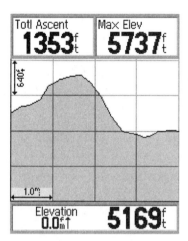

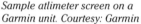

Sample atlimeter screen on a Garmin unit. Courtesy: Garmin

Garmin GPSMAP 76S. Courtesy: Garmin.

> **An elevation computer** that offers current elevation, re-settable minimum and maximum elevation, ascent/descent rate, total ascent/descent, average and maximum ascent/descent rate.

> **Local pressure readings** (mbar/inches HG) and 12-hour automatic pressure trend recording.

Garmin's Rino GPS receivers have 8 to 24 MB of internal memory (Rino 120 and 130 only) and come preloaded with the America's Highway base map. The innovative feature for outdoor activities is the incorporation of a two-way hand-held radio with a transmission range of up to 5 miles, or up to 14 miles on the more fully enhanced 520 HCx and 530HCx. In addition to voice communications, the radio permits you to see the location of another unit on your screen.

Garmin's Rino 130 (L) and Rino 530 HCx (R) have two-way radio capability. Courtesy: Garmin

FUTURE GPS DEVELOPMENTS

If you've watched a *Star Trek* rerun lately you may recall that ingenious TriCorder device that serves in a multitude of roles, including as a long-range communicator, navigational aid, and comprehensive sensor array and analysis tool; it also features a database bigger than the Encyclopedia Britannica. We may not see all those features soon, but integrated units that incorporate all the features of a PDA, cell phone, and GPS—*plus* wireless Web access for email, browsing, and map downloads—are available now. Some incorporate MP3 music playing capability, a voice recorder, and even a basic digital camera. Units with environmental sensors will likely appear soon. Specialized units are available to meet the specific needs of military, industrial, and commercial users. The biggest difference between most of them and a TriCorder is that they are smaller and better looking.

GPS capability is rapidly becoming a normal part of many facets of commerce and our daily lives. As price and size plummet and accuracy increases, the technology will be used to locate and track more and more things. There will be no way to avoid it.

Common GPS Receivers

There is a sizable number of GPS receivers on the market. Many are designed for special applications, such as surveying. Those listed here are handheld units generally intended for outdoor recreational use. All GPS receivers listed here have at least 12 channels. That is, they are capable of receiving signals from 12 different GPS satellites simultaneously.

Basic Handheld Units

Manu-facturer	Model	Channels	Way-points	Routes/Tracks	Coordinates	Battery	Temperature	Map	Features	List	Street	Comments
Garmin	eTrex H	12	500	10	Lat/Long, UTM/UPS, Maidenheas, MGRS, and other grids	2 AA, up to 17 hours continuous	5 to 158°F	n/a	Hunt/fish calendar, sun and moon information	$106	$85	
	Foretrex 101	12	500	10	Lat/Long, UTM/UPS, Maidenheas, MGRS, and other grids	2 AA, up to 15 hours continuous	5 to 158°F	n/a	Wrist mounted with hunt/fish calendar, sun and moon information	$138	$101	waterproof
	Foretrex 102	12	500	10	Lat/Long, UTM/UPS, Maidenheas, MGRS, and other grids	rechargeable internal Lithium-ion battery up to 15 hours	5 to 158°F	n/a	Wrist mounted with hunt/fish calendar, sun and moon information	$182	$132	waterproof
	Geko 201	12	500	10	Lat/Long, UTM/UPS, Maidenheas, MGRS, and other grids	2 AAA up to 12 hours	5 to 158°F	n/a	Hunt/fish calendar, sun and moon information, outdoor GPS games	$150	$125	
	Geko 301	12	500	10	Lat/Long, UTM/UPS, Maidenheas, MGRS, and other grids	2 AAA up to 9 hours	5 to 158°F	n/a	Hunt/fish calendar, sun and moon information, outdoor GPS games, electronic compass, barometric altimeter, area calculation	$246	$190	
	GPS 60	12	500	20	Lat/Long, UTM/UPS, Maidenheas, MGRS, and other grids	2 AA up to 28 hours	5 to 158°F	n/a	Hunt/fish calendar, sun and moon information, outdoor GPS games, electronic compass, barometric altimeter, area calculation	$192	$180	also feature geocaching mode
	GPS 72	12	500	10	Lat/Long, UTM/UPS, Maidenheas, MGRS, and other grids	2 AA up to 16 hours	5 to 158°F	n/a	Hunt/fish calendar, sun and moon information, tide tables, area calculation	$130	$109	waterproof & floats
	GPS 76	12	500	10	Lat/Long, UTM/UPS, Maidenheas, MGRS, and other grids	2 AA up to 16 hours	5 to 158°F	n/a	Hunt/fish calendar, sun and moon information, tide tables, area calculation	$180	$160	waterproof & floats
Magellan	eXplorist 100	14	500	3	Lat/Long, UTM, MGRS, OSGB, and other grids	2 AA up to 18 hours	5 to 158°F	n/a	compass	$110	$110	water resistant
Teletype	Bluetooth GPS	20				rechargeable internal Lithium-ion battery up to 55 hours	minus 10 to 60°C	sold separately		$129		
	20 Channel Sirf III Bluetooth	20				replaceable Lithium-ion rechargeable battery up to 10 hours	minus 10 to 60°C	sold separately		$89		

Mapping Units

Manu-facturer	Model	Channels	Way-points	Routes/Tracks	Coordinates	Battery	Temperature	Map	Features	List	Street	Comments
Brunton	Atlas MNS GPS	12	1000	10	Lat/Long	2 AA, up to 2 weeks	−13 to 158°F	Built in US & Hawaii background—expandable mapping with optional memory cards	barometer, altimeter, digital compass	$399	$284	24 hr pressure history, 12 hr weather forecast, high-low elevation
Garmin	Colorado 300	12	1000	20	Lat/Long, UTM/UPS, Maidenheas, MGRS, and other grids	2 AA or 2 NiMH up to 15 hours	5 to 158°F	World wide basemap included other maps available as optional downloads	Auto routing feature, electronic compass, barometric altimeter, geocaching mode, GPS games, hunt/fish calendar, sun, moon, & tide tables, many other features	$532	$500	waterproof

Manufacturer	Model	Channels	Waypoints	Routes/Tracks	Coordinates	Battery	Temperature	Map	Features	List	Street	Comments
	Colorado 400c	12	1000	20	Lat/Long, UTM/UPS, Maidenheas, MGRS, and other grids	2 AA or 2 NiMH up to 15 hours	5 to 158°F	Multiple preloaded maps	Auto routing feature, electronic compass, barometric altimeter, geocaching mode, GPS games, hunt/fish calendar, sun, moon, & tide tables, many other features	$640	$599	waterproof
	Colorado 400i	12	1000	20	Lat/Long, UTM/UPS, Maidenheas, MGRS, and other grids	2 AA or 2 NiMH up to 15 hours	5 to 158°F	Multiple preloaded maps	Auto routing feature, electronic compass, barometric altimeter, geocaching mode, GPS games, hunt/fish calendar, sun, moon, & tide tables, many other features	$640	$599	waterproof
	Colorado 400t	12	1000	20	Lat/Long, UTM/UPS, Maidenheas, MGRS, and other grids	2 AA or 2 NiMH up to 15 hours	5 to 158°F	Multiple preloaded maps (including topographic)	Auto routing feature, electronic compass, barometric altimeter, geocaching mode, GPS games, hunt/fish calendar, sun, moon, & tide tables, many other features	$640	$599	waterproof
	eTrex Summit HC	12	1000	10	Lat/Long, UTM/UPS, Maidenheas, MGRS, and other grids	2 AA up to 14 hours	5 to 158°F	Basemap	Electronic compass, barometric altimeter, geocaching mode, GPS games, hunt/fish calendar, sun & moon tables, other features	$246	$172	waterproof
	eTrex Venture HC	12	500	10	Lat/Long, UTM/UPS, Maidenheas, MGRS, and other grids	2 AA, up to 14 hours	5 to 158°F	Basemap	Geocaching mode, GPS games, hunt/fish calendar, sun & moon tables, other features	$182	$127	waterproof
	eTrex Legend	12	1000	10	Lat/Long, UTM/UPS, Maidenheas, MGRS, and other grids	2 AA, up to 18 hours	5 to 158°F	Basemap	Hunt/fish calendar, sun & moon tables, other features	$160	$135	waterproof
	eTrex Legend HCx	12	1000	20	Lat/Long, UTM/UPS, Maidenheas, MGRS, and other grids	2 AA, up to 25 hours	5 to 158°F	Basemap	Auto routing, hunt/fish calendar, sun & moon tables, other features	$267	$238	waterproof
	eTrex Vista	12	1000	20	Lat/Long, UTM/UPS, Maidenheas, MGRS, and other grids	2 AA, up to 12 hours	5 to 158°F	Basemap—other downloadable maps available	Electronic compass, barometric altimeter, hunt/fish calendar, sun & moon tables, other features	$214	$190	waterproof
	eTrex Vista HCx	12	1000	20	Lat/Long, UTM/UPS, Maidenheas, MGRS, and other grids	2 AA, up to 25 hours	5 to 158°F	Basemap	Auto routing feature, electronic compass, barometric altimeter, geocaching mode, GPS games, hunt/fish calendar, sun & moon tables, many other features	$321	$240	waterproof
	GPS Map 60	12	500	20	Lat/Long, UTM/UPS, Maidenheas, MGRS, and other grids	2 AA, up to 28 hours	5 to 158°F	Basemap—other downloadable maps available	Geocaching mode, GPS games, hunt/fish calendar, sun & moon tables, other features	$250	$190	waterproof
	GPS Map 60Cx	12	1000	20	Lat/Long, UTM/UPS, Maidenheas, MGRS, and other grids	2 AA, up to 18 hours	5 to 158°F	Basemap—other downloadable maps available	Geocaching mode, GPS games, hunt/fish calendar, sun & moon tables, other features	$375	$299	waterproof

Manufacturer	Model	Channels	Waypoints	Routes/Tracks	Coordinates	Battery	Temperature	Map	Features	List	Street	Comments
	GPS Map 60SCx	12	1000	20	Lat/Long, UTM/UPS, Maidenheas, MGRS, and other grids	2 AA, up to 18 hours	5 to 158°F	Basemap—other down-loadable maps available	Auto routing feature, electronic compass, barometric altimeter, geocaching mode, GPS games, hunt/fish calendar, sun & moon tables, many other features	$428	$399	waterproof
	GPS Map 76	12	500	10	Lat/Long, UTM/UPS, Maidenheas, MGRS, and other grids	2 AA, up to 16 hours	5 to 158°F	Basemap—other down-loadable maps available	Hunt/fish calendar, sun & moon tables, other features	$200	$169	waterproof
	GPS 76S	12	500	50	Lat/Long, UTM/UPS, Maidenheas, MGRS, and other grids	2 AA, up to 16 hours	5 to 158°F	Basemap—other down-loadable maps available	Electronic compass, barometric altimeter, hunt/fish calendar, sun & moon tables, many other features	$250	$209	waterproof
	GPS 76Cx	12	1000	20	Lat/Long, UTM/UPS, Maidenheas, MGRS, and other grids	2 AA, up to 18 hours	5 to 158°F	Basemap—other down-loadable maps available	Auto routing feature, geocaching mode, GPS games, hunt/fish calendar, sun & moon tables, many other features	$375	$318	waterproof & floats
	GPS 76 CSX	12	1000	20	Lat/Long, UTM/UPS, Maidenheas, MGRS, and other grids	2 AA, up to 18 hours	5 to 158°F	Basemap—other down-loadable maps available	Auto routing feature, electronic compass, barometric altimeter, geocaching mode, GPS games, hunt/fish calendar, sun & moon tables, many other features	$428	$312	waterproof & floats
Magellan	Triton 1500	20			Lat/Long & UTM	2 AA, up to 10 hours	14 to 140°F	Basemap—other down-loadable maps available	Built-in flashlight, voice recorder	$400	$349	waterproof
	Triton 200	20			Lat/Long & UTM	2 AA, up to 10 hours	14 to 140°F	Basemap—other down-loadable maps available	Compass screen	$130	$119	water resistant
	Triton 300	20			Lat/Long & UTM	2 AA, up to 10 hours	14 to 140°F	Basemap—other down-loadable maps available	Compass screen	$150	$129	waterproof
	Triton 400	20			Lat/Long & UTM	2 AA, up to 10 hours	14 to 140°F	Basemap—other down-loadable maps available		$200	$146	waterproof
	Triton 500	20			Lat/Long & UTM	2 AA, up to 10 hours	14 to 140°F	Basemap—other down-loadable maps available	Electronic compass & barometer	$250	$199	waterproof
	Triton 2000	20			Lat/Long & UTM	2 AA, up to 10 hours	14 to 140°F	Basemap—other down-loadable maps available	Camera, Voice recorder, compass, barometer	$500	$429	water resistant
	Crossover	20				Lithium-ion rechargeable, up to 8 hours continuous	14 to 140°F	Basemap—other down-loadable maps available		$400	$358	
Teletype	GPS v. 3.0 WAAS	12				3 volt Lithium battery	32 to 158°F	Downloadable software maps—extra		$199		

Manufacturer	Model	Channels	Way-points	Routes/Tracks	Coordinates	Battery	Temperature	Map	Features	List	Street	Comments
DeLorme	PN-20	12				2 AA batteries	minus 20 to 158°C	Basemap—other downloadable maps available		$400	varies with maps	waterproof
Lowrance	iFinder Expedition C	16	1000			2 AA up to 14 hours		Basemap—other downloadable maps available	Electronic compass, barometric altimeter, other features	$300	$229	waterproof
	iFinder Hunt C	16	2000			2 AA up to 16 hours		Basemap—other downloadable maps available	Electronic compass, barometric altimeter, other features	$350	$319	waterproof
	iFinder Hunt	12	2000			2 AA up to 12 hours		Basemap—other downloadable maps available	Electronic compass, barometric altimeter, other features	$300	$254	waterproof
	iFinder H2O C	16	1000			2 AA up to 14 hours		Basemap—other downloadable maps available	Electronic compass, barometric altimeter, other features	$250	$230	waterproof
	iFinder H2O	12	1000			2 AA up to 12 hours		Basemap—other downloadable maps available		$250	$230	waterproof
	iFinder G20	16	1000			2 AA up to 50 hours		Basemap—other downloadable maps available				

GPS With Two-Way Radio

Manufacturer	Model	Channels	Way-points	Routes/Tracks	Coordinates	Battery	Temperature	Map	Features	List	Street	Comments
Garmin	Rino 110	12	500	20	Lat/Long, UTM/UPS, Maidenheas, MGRS, and other grids	3 AA up to 14 hours	minus 4 to 158°C	n/a	Hunt/fish calendar, sun/moon tables other features—2 mile radio range	$195	$150	waterproof
	Rino 120	12	500	20	Lat/Long, UTM/UPS, Maidenheas, MGRS, and other grids	3 AA up to 14 hours	minus 4 to 158°C	Basemap—other downloadable maps available	Hunt/fish calendar, sun/moon tables other features—2 mile radio range	$268	$178	waterproof
	Rino 130	12	500	20	Lat/Long, UTM/UPS, Maidenheas, MGRS, and other grids	3 AA up to 14 hours	minus 4 to 158°C	Basemap—other downloadable maps available	Electronic compass, barometric altimeter, hunt/fish calendar, sun/moon tables, other features—2 mile radio range	$375	$349	waterproof
	Rino 520H Cx	12	500	20	Lat/Long, UTM/UPS, Maidenheas, MGRS, and other grids	Rechargeable lithium-ion battery up to 14 hours	minus 4 to 140°C	Basemap—other downloadable maps available	Hunt/fish calendar, sun/moon tables other features—2 mile radio range	$482	$337	waterproof
	Rino 530HCx	12	500	20	Lat/Long, UTM/UPS, Maidenheas, MGRS, and other grids	Rechargeable lithium-ion battery up to 14 hours	minus 4 to 140°C	Basemap—other downloadable maps available	Electronic compass, barometric altimeter, hunt/fish calendar, sun/moon tables, other features—2 mile radio range	$536	$462	waterproof

CHAPTER 3

➤ Maps: Reducing a Sphere to a Flat Surface

A GPS receiver can give us our location, the correct time, and if we are moving, our speed. Usually we want to determine our position relative to other things around us, and the most common way to do this is to use a map. In the more advanced GPS receivers, the map may be an integral part of the display if the receiver is linked to an external personal digital assistant (PDA) or notebook computer the position signal can also be displayed directly on a map. If we are simply traveling down a highway, this may be enough. For the outdoorsman, however, a more detailed understanding of maps will make the GPS receiver a much more useful tool. In this chapter we'll discuss some of the basic features of maps and their construction. We'll also look at the various types of maps that are most useful in the outdoors.

THE SIZE AND SHAPE OF PLANET EARTH

How big is planet earth and just how round is it? How can we accurately define where we are on its surface, and how can we translate the position information from a GPS receiver to a location on a flat map? Why is the equator where it is and why is 0° longitude located where it is? The answers are not as elementary as you might suppose.

Planet earth, dubbed by TV culture as the third rock from the sun, is an oblate sphere with a circumference at the equator of 24,901.55 miles (40,075.16 kilometers), compared to a circumference of 24,859.82 miles (40,008 kilometers) for a vertical ring passing through both poles. Thus, the earth is 0.168 percent greater in circumference at the equator than around the poles. You might think of it as a basketball when someone rests a foot on top of it. The bulge at the equator is the result of gravitational pull from the moon and sun.

Note that modern measurements yield a slightly different value for the polar circumference than the originally intended 40 million meters (used as the definition of a meter).

If we add the height of the world's tallest mountain, Mount Everest at 29,092 feet (8,867 meters), and the depth of the deepest ocean, in the Marianas Trench near Guam, which is 35,839 feet (10,924 meters), we find that the earth's surface varies by about 0.155 percent of its diameter. These small percentages may make the earth seem essentially like a perfectly round sphere, but the differences are enough to complicate accurate mapmaking and accurate navigation.

DATUMS AND ELLIPSOIDS

Geodetic datums are mathematical descriptions of the size and shape of the earth and the origin and orientation of coordinate systems used to construct maps. Early datums assumed the earth was a perfect sphere, but modern satellite measurements have produced much more accurate datums. The important consideration for GPS users is that the datum setting of the GPS be the same as whatever map is being used, electronic or paper. Use of coordinate locations from maps or instruments in differing datums can result in errors of hundreds of meters. On the open ocean or a vast desert expanse, this might not be significant, but for many outdoor activities we want, and need, to be more precise.

The Global Positioning System uses the World Geodetic System 1984 datum (WGS-84). Up-to-date U. S. Geological Survey (USGS) maps generally use NAD-83 (which is the same as WGS84), but many older maps use the North American Datum of 1927 (NAD-27). Even though GPS receivers use WGS-84, they can translate that data to almost any map datum. If you're using a map, make sure your GPS receiver is set to same datum.

GRIDS THAT DEFINE LOCATION

To help us find our exact location on a map, a number of coordinate systems or grids have been developed. Most GPS receivers will work with several different map grids and, as we will see, each set of grids has certain advantages that make it useful for some applications. Common terms useful for understanding grid systems are defined in the sidebar below.

All lines of longitude are circles of the same size—okay, almost the same size. The equator is the biggest circle of latitude. As you move toward the pole, the circles get smaller, until at 90° N or S it is only a point. If you have trouble remembering which kind of lines run in which direction, just remember that the o in longitude is always the same size.

LONGITUDE AND LATITUDE

The longitude/latitude grid is one of the most common grid systems. Most people are at least vaguely familiar with the terms, and longitude/latitude grids are printed on almost all maps.

Rotational Axis: An imaginary line, pole-to-pole, around which the earth revolves.

Equator: The equator is the circle on the surface of the earth farthest from the rotational axis. Each point on the circle is equidistant from the North and South Poles.

Prime Meridian: A meridian is a north-south line on the surface of the earth. The prime meridian is the 0 point for longitude on earth. In 1884 the position of the large "Transit Circle" telescope in the British Royal Observatory in Greenwich, England, was arbitrarily designated the prime meridian (longitude 0°, by definition, and latitude 51° 28'38" N). All locations are measured east and west of this line.

Latitude refers to an angular distance from the equator to any point on the surface of the earth as measured north or south of the equator. The equator is latitude 0°, the North Pole is latitude 90° N (north), and the South Pole is latitude 90° S (south). One degree of latitude is approximately equal to 69 miles (110 km). The value increases slightly as we move toward the poles due to the "squashed" shape of the earth near the poles. A line of constant latitude is one that circles the earth parallel to the equator and at a specific distance north or south of the equator.

Longitude refers to an angular distance on the surface of the earth, measured along any latitude line east or west of the prime meridian. A meridian of longitude is a vertical line on the surface of the earth passing from pole to pole. By international agreement, the meridian that passes through the original site of the Royal Greenwich Observatory at Greenwich, England, is designated the prime meridian. All points on the prime meridian, whether north or south of it, are at 0° longitude. Points on the earth east or west of the prime meridian have longitudes ranging from 0° to 180° E (east) or 0° to 180° W (west), respectively. The 180° meridian lies on the other side of the earth and is exactly opposite the prime meridian. Except for places where it is moved slightly east or west to avoid populated areas, the international date line lies along the 180° meridian.

Thus, parallels of latitude and meridians of longitude together form a grid that allows us to specify the coordinates of any position on the earth's surface.

Although so far we have talked about longitude and latitude as angles in degrees measured from the equator and prime meridian, it turns out that we will need more accurate angle measurements in order to accurately locate points on the surface of the earth. As you may recall, an angle is just a method of subdividing a circle. A complete circle is divided into 360°. In the case of longitude and latitude angles, we use values that range only between 0° and 180°, since we also add the N or S and E or W notation to them. However, remember that earlier we pointed out that one degree of latitude was approximately equal to 69 miles. (One degree of longitude is also approximately 69 miles at the equator, but due to the way longitude meridians are constructed, this distance decreases rapidly as we approach either pole.) Now suppose that we happen to be out in the ocean somewhere on the equator (for simplicity), and that we know our latitude and longitude to within plus or minus 1°. This tells us that we are located within an area roughly 138 miles (69 miles × 2) by 138 miles or roughly somewhere within an area of 19,044 square miles. That's not a very exact location, especially if we are in trouble and need a rescue ship to come to our aid!

This example points out the obvious need for us to be able to specify our latitude and longitude in units smaller than degrees, if our position is to have any real meaning. There are several ways in which this is done.

The simplest way, although not commonly used, is to express the exact longitude and latitude angles in decimal fractions. For example, a specific location might be given as: W 117.495° (longitude), N 34.857° (latitude). The latitude value is typically written first, followed by the longitude, but to be consistent with other coordinate systems the X value, longitude, should be written first. Obviously, we can give our position more accurately by including more digits to the right of the decimal point.

A more commonly used approach is to subdivide each degree into smaller segments. One subdivision is a minute, which is denoted by a single tick mark ('). Degrees and minutes are related as follows:

$$1° = 60'$$

One degree equals 60 minutes, or 1 minute equals ⅟₆₀ of a degree. In this format a particular location, in terms of longitude and latitude, may be given as:

$$W\ 72°\ 57.23'N\ 53°\ 27.41'$$

Note that we have expressed the minute values in decimal fractions. Just as we subdivided a degree into minutes, we can also subdivide a minute up into smaller units called seconds and denoted by a double tick mark ("). Minutes and seconds are related as follows:

$$1' = 60"$$

One minute equals 60 seconds, or 1 second equals $\frac{1}{60}$ of a minute. It also follows directly from these two definitions that 1 degree equals 3600 seconds (60 × 60) and that 1 second equals $\frac{1}{3,600}$ of a degree. In this format, we can express a set of coordinates as:

$$\text{W } 117° \ 49' \ 36" \ \text{N } 34° \ 06'43"$$

By remembering the relationships among degrees, minutes, and seconds we can easily convert latitude and longitude positions from one format to another with a little practice.

Longitude and latitude notation can appear in several formats. In addition to degrees-minutes-seconds (degminsec or DMS), degrees—decimal minutes (degmindec or DMD) and Decimal Degrees (decdeg or DD) are common. Decimal notation simplifies calculations but seldom transfers easily to paper maps marked in DMS. Our office door is at the following location:

degminsec	95° 14' 12" W 38° 58' 9" N
degmindec	95° 14.20' W 38° 58.15'N
degdec	95.23689° W 38.96944° N

Many mapping software packages and related Web pages have conversion routines that allow you to enter one grid format and datum and convert it to one or more other formats and datums.

UNIVERSAL TRANSVERSE MERCATOR (UTM)

The National Imagery and Mapping Agency (NIMA), formerly known as the Defense Mapping Agency, developed the Universal Transverse Mercator (UTM) grid system. It is widely used to define two-dimensional horizontal positions on the earth's surface. Its principal advantage is simplicity: No degrees, minutes, seconds; no 1/60 increments; and no negative numbers. Some older GPS units are not capable of displaying UTM coordinates, and some older maps are not marked with them. Avoid both if possible. UTM is easier than latitude/longitude and with a little practice it becomes very intuitive.

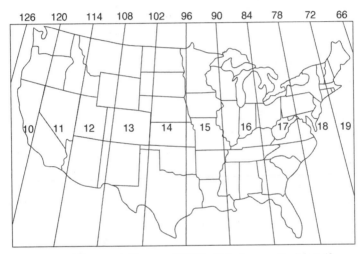

The Universal Transverse Mercator (UTM) grid that covers the lower 48 United States comprises 10 zones—from zone 10 on the west coast through zone 19 in New England.

The UTM grid divides the earth's surface into 6° wide longitudinal (vertical) strips extending from 80° South latitude to 84° North latitude. These strips are perpendicular to the equator and are labeled with a zone number. Zone 01 begins at the international date line (180° East and West longitude) and extends eastward to 6° West longitude, centered on 3° West longitude. Moving from west to east, each successive vertical zone is centered on the next 6° of longitude, wrapping around the world until zone 60 meets zone 01.

Beginning at 80° South latitude and extending to 84° North latitude the UTM grid divides the earth's surface horizontally into 8° wide bands. The southernmost band, centered on 76° South latitude, is labeled with a designator, the letter C, and successive bands moving from south to north move through the alphabet, ending at X. Unlike all other horizontal bands, X is 12° wide, extending from 72° North to 84° North. There is no O designator to avoid confusion with the number zero (0). Using the UTM grid system, two numbers (the vertical zone) and one letter (the horizontal zone) designate a specific 6° wide and 8° high rectangle across all the sections of our planet that most would consider inhabitable. If someone tells you they live in UTM PO4, for instance, you know they are from Hawaii.

By definition, the distance from the equator to the geographic North Pole is 10,000,000 meters (it varies slightly). The equator is 0° latitude, and the pole is 90° latitude (North or South). Therefore, each degree of latitude is equal to 111,111.11 meters, and north-to-south dimension of each UTM zone would be 888,888.89 meters (51.31 miles) for zones C through W The circumference of the earth at the equator is 40,075.16 km (24,901.55 miles), making a 6° UTM zone there 667,919 meters (415.0 miles east to west). In horizontal zone S—which covers the central United States—the curvature of the earth has reduced the east-west distance at the central latitude of 36° to around 539,300 meters (335.1 miles). At the northern edge of the grid in zone X, the east-to-west dimension declines to 69,660 meters (43.3 miles). All these distances are approximate, because this general description does not yet incorporate adjustments for the earth's exact shape.

Each UTM grid zone is further divided vertically and horizontally, using a convention that avoids negative numbers, in a manner that can be extended literally down to the head of a pin. The grid origin is placed at the lower left-hand corner of the zone cell, and the central longitude (vertical) is assigned a value of 500,000. All locations are given by X and Y coordinates from the origin in the lower left-hand corner. Note that we are always describing a point located east (X value or easting) and north (Y value or northing) from the origin. Why 500,000 for the X value of the central longitude? Recall that the horizontal east-to-west dimension of a vertical 6° wide UTM zone at the equator was about 667,919 meters. Half that distance is 333,960 meters. If the X value at the origin is 166,040 meters and we travel east 333,960 meters, we arrive at 500,000, and no negative values occur. We could use 350,000, but 500,000 is easier to remember.

The UTM grid value assigned to this point of origin is the distance from the equator in meters of the latitude of the south side of the zone. Where we live in zone S, which begins at 32° North latitude, the zone origin begins at 32 × 111, 111. 111, or 3555556 northing.

STATE PLANE COORDINATE SYSTEM

The State Plane Coordinate System (SPCS) was implemented in the United States in the 1930s when the U. S. Coast and Geodetic Survey used it to provide a common reference system to mappers and surveyors. Later, in the 1950s, the U.S. Geological Survey began basing new topographic quadrangles on it. SPCS divides the 50 states and the U.S. Caribbean islands into more than 120 numbered sections. These sections, referred to as zones, have assigned code numbers that define the projection parameters for that region. SPSC coordinate values are printed on many USGS maps, but they are of limited value to the outdoors person taking advantage of GPS technology. The typical map user will find it easier to stick with lat/long and UTM.

MILITARY GRID REFERENCE SYSTEM

The Military Grid Reference System (MGRS) is an extension of the UTM system. The UTM zone number and zone character are used to identify an area that is 6° wide east to west

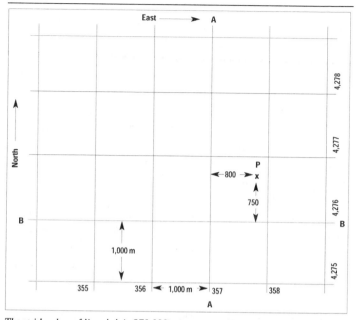

The grid value of line A-A is 370,000 meters east. The grid value of line B-B is 4,276,000 meters north. Point B is 800 meters east and 750 meters north of the grid lines; therefore, the grid coordinates of point P are north 4,276,000 and east 370,000.

and 8° north and south. The UTM zone number and designator are followed by 100-kilometer-square easting and northing identifiers. The MGRS system uses a set of alphabetic characters to designate each of the 100-kilometer grid squares. The designation scheme starts at the 180° meridian and uses the characters A to Z (omitting I and O) for 18°, after which the system starts over. Proceeding north from the equator, the characters A to V (again omitting I and O) are used to designate the 100-kilometer squares, repeating every 2,000 kilometers. Northing designators usually begin with A at the equator for odd-numbered UTM easting zones. In the even-numbered easting zones the northing designators are offset by five characters, which start at the equator with F. The zones south of the equator are designated by characters set in the same pattern used north of the equator.

The UTM zone number, UTM zone, and the two 100-kilometer-square characters are followed by an even number of numeric characters representing easting and northing values. If 10 numeric characters are used, a precision of 1 meter is assumed. Two numeric characters imply a precision of 10 kilometers. As the number of numeric characters increases from 2 to 10, the precision changes from 10 kilometers to 1 kilometer, 100 meters, 10 meters, and finally 1 meter.

PUBLIC LAND SURVEY SYSTEM

Your GPS unit will not list your location in the Public Land Survey System (PLSS), but understanding how it works will sometimes make finding where you want to go easier. PLSS is the common system for describing the size and location of rural land across most of the United States except for the 13 original colonies, Texas, and Hawaii. When folks tell you, "We have a great hunting lease you can use. It's the S ½, S 23 T 4 N R 14 W 6th PM down in Franklin County," they are talking PLSS. We mention this system because of its relationship to landownership and because of the tremendous imprint it has left on the natural landscape.

In the PLSS, there are 31 principal meridians (PMs; north-south lines) and baselines (BLs; east-west lines) in the contiguous United States. The intersection of these lines is known as the initial point. Some meridians are numbered, such as the Sixth Principal Meridian, while others are named, such as the New Mexico Principal Meridian.

Townships are numbered north or south of the baseline ranges, or a "column" of townships is numbered east or west of the principal meridian. For example, T4N, R5E NM Principal Meridian is the fourth "row" of townships north of the BL and is in the fifth "column" east of the PM.

The Wisconsin Department of Natural Resources has a very useful concise tutorial on PLSS at http://www.dnr.state.wi.us/org/land/forestry/Private/PLSSTut/plsstutl.htm. The PLSS divides Wisconsin at the fourth Principal Meridian, located at 90° West longitude.

Initially, no allowance was made for convergence and accumulated error; after some modifications, however, this error was placed in the north and west portions of a township. In theory, each section (1 square mile) contains 640 acres, but errors and convergence may cause discrepancies. Each 6-mile-square township is divided into 36 sections (640 acres apiece). Numbering begins in the northeast corner section (1) and ends in the southeast corner section (36). The numbers run in alternate lines east to west and then west to east, et cetera.

Each section may be subdivided into smaller parcels (aliquot parts). For example, a 10-acre parcel could be described as: SE 1/4 SE 1/4 SE 1/4 sec. 5, T2N, R3W Boise Meridian, Idaho. Translated into lay terms, this means: the southeast quarter of the southeast quarter of the southeast quarter of section 5, Township 2 North, Range 3 West of the Boise Meridian. Descriptions are read left to right, but locating them is easier if you read right to left or from larger division to smaller.

Each quadrant of a section (NE, NW, SW, SE) can be subdivided using this method. Further subdivision below 10 acres is usually by metes and bounds.

Periodically, due to convergence (24 miles), township lines are adjusted: Every 24 miles from the baseline, a standard parallel or correction line is used to correct for longitudinal convergence. Adjustments are also made when the system contacts other survey systems such as earlier methods, tribal lands, land grants (say, Spanish grants in New Mexico), and bodies of water. In these cases the previous survey takes precedence, and the section lines end at the boundaries of such.

The surveying manuals required specific monuments for township and section corners. Today the BLM uses a stainless-steel pipe with a bronze cap, but earlier monuments can be stone, posts, or dirt mounds. When possible, corners are further referenced to bearing trees or other natural features.

Witness and bearing trees and line blazes also help relocate points.

The chain is the unit of measurement for the PLSS. Although this unit may not be familiar to you, surveys of public lands retain this old unit. Except for some mineral and town site surveys, all are horizontal chain measurements. The basic features of the PLSS chain measurement system are listed in the following table.

PLSS CHAIN UNITS OF MEASUREMENTS

1 chain = 100 links or 66 feet

1 link = 7.92 inches

80 chains = 1 mile or 5,280 feet

480 chains = 6 miles or a township line

1 acre = 10 square chains or 43,560 square feet

Surveyors were and are required to keep detailed field notes and prepare plats of the survey. The plat is a legal document that establishes boundaries and ownership. In court, an original monument position, even one in error, usually takes precedence.

MAP PROJECTIONS AND SCALES

The earth is a sphere, but maps, excluding globes, are flat. Although we may cut a cylinder apart lengthwise and lay it out flat without distortion—imagine, for example, doing this with the label on a can of soup—we cannot cut apart a sphere and lay the pieces flat without some distortion. A map projection is a mathematical transformation that allows us to relate the coordinates of a point on a spherical surface, like the earth, to another set of coordinates on a flat surface, such as a map. Distortion is an inevitable consequence of trying to project the points on a spherical surface onto a flat plane. Angles, areas, directions, shapes, and distances can all become distorted when transformed from a spherical surface to a flat plane. A number of different map projections have been designed, each intended to minimize the amount of distortion in one of the above properties. Unfortunately, when the amount of distortion in one of the above properties—for example, angles—is corrected, the remaining properties become even more distorted. All map projections are thus compromises. The particular projection chosen is the one that most closely fits the purposes of the particular map. There are a number of widely used map projections. The Mercator projection, for example, is the one we commonly see on world maps. This projection preserves angles, but as we move away from the equator, distances become progressively distorted. On these maps Greenland appears to be larger than South America, though in reality the area of South America is nine times larger than that of Greenland.

Map scales refer to the relationships between the distances on a map and the corresponding distances on the surface of the earth. Scales are expressed as either a fraction or a ratio and are assigned fixed values for each specific map. Map scales may be large or small. A large-scale map would show a small area but in great detail. Similarly, a small-scale map would show a large area but with only a minimal amount of detail.

Map scale ratios are expressed as two numbers separated by a colon, such as 1:10,000. This scale would indicate that 1 unit of measurement on a map—which may be an inch or centimeter, or any other unit—represents 10,000 of the same units on the actual surface of the earth. The larger the value of the second number of the ratio, the smaller the map scale. Large-scale maps have ratios of 1:24,000 or greater. Intermediate-scale maps have ratios between 1:50,000 and 1:100,000, and small-scale maps have ratios smaller than 1:250,000.

GRID AND MEASUREMENT CONVERSION TOOLS

How to Convert Decimal Degrees into Degrees, Minutes, Seconds http://www.geography.about.com/0962932697.htm

Geodetic Calculation Methods
http://www.auslig.gov.au/.../calcs.htm

Conversion between Ellipsoidal and Grid Coordinates
http://www.anzlic.org.au/.../chapter5.htm

Units of Measure Conversions
http://www.grouptravels.com/.../uom.htm

Measurement Conversion Factors
http://www.iol.ie/.../measurehtm

CHAPTER 4

Land Navigation

While GPS receivers can make finding your way in the great outdoors almost as easy as turning on a pocket radio, a certain degree of skill in the more traditional methods of land navigation will allow you to use your GPS receiver more effectively and is important in the unlikely event that your GPS unit fails. We discuss some of the basic principles of land navigation in this chapter.

KEEPING TRACK OF WHERE YOU ARE

The best way to avoid getting lost is to persistently keep track of where you are. Ship captains do it, and airplane pilots do it—or they have a designated navigator to do it for them. They maintain a track on a map of where they started, what course they traveled, and at what speed. Speed × time = distance traveled. They consistently maintain an estimated position, which they correct with navigational "fixes" at regular intervals. It's much easier to do on land than in the air or at sea, where wind and/or currents must be taken into account. The process is often dubbed dead reckoning (DR). No doubt nautical, the origins of the term are clouded in history, but to a sailor dead means "exact." Some assert the term actually comes from a simple method of measuring a ship's speed through the water. A floating object thrown over at the bow was dead or fixed in the water. The time it took for the object to reach the stern could be converted to ship's speed. A dead run is a straight track downwind to a specific destination. For reckoning to work at sea, it must be exact, requiring careful and continuous attention to course, time, speed, wind, and currents.

THE ADMIRAL OF THE OCEAN SEA

Half a century ago, most schoolchildren were taught that Christopher Columbus discovered America while searching for a shorter route to India and that he accomplished this remarkable feat because he was one of few people who understood that the earth was round. He simply blindly sailed west, not fearing that he would fall off the flat world. As Samuel Morison points out in his Pulitzer Prize-winning *Admiral of the Ocean Sea*, however, no capable sea captain of Columbus's era thought the earth was flat, and Columbus was a capable captain and an exceptional dead-reckoning navigator. Celestial navigation was not widely understood and Columbus's tools, knowledge, and skills were meager, but he knew how to maintain a track. He crossed an ocean unknown to him, found his way home, and found his way back again. He kept track of course and speed with a simple compass and a floating block. The critical facts that Columbus didn't have were the size of the earth, and the knowledge that the western route was actually the longer path to India (not to mention there being two continents in the way). The actual size of the earth, while still debated in the late 15th century, wasn't exactly a secret. The Greek Eratosthenes had made a pretty good calculation in the third century B.C., and many others had followed. This knowledge was likely available to the advisers King Ferdinand selected to evaluate Columbus's proposal. They concluded the distance was too far and recommended against funding the venture. Columbus had his own calculations—some suspect he may have adjusted them in his favor—and Queen Isabella overruled. The rest is, as they say, history.

Columbus's reputation has been tarnished a bit by evidence that many other non-Natives made it to North America before he did, some saying he didn't really "discover" it at all. While others, including the Norse and (according to some) even the Chinese, beat Columbus to the New World, to him alone can we trace the permanent "modern" settlement of it by people of other continents, much to the chagrin and detriment of the Native Americans.

THE JOURNEY OF DISCOVERY

Just over 300 years after Columbus (re)discovered North America, a group of explorers with much more sophisticated navigational knowledge and tools set out to learn more about the continent. In May 1804, Meriwether Lewis and William Clark departed St. Louis area in what is now the state of Missouri with 40-some other men in a group named the Corps of Discovery. They returned almost two and a half years later, in September 1806, having traveled more than 8,000 miles to the Pacific Ocean and back through territory largely unknown to Europeans. These were not just a couple of guys and their buddies going up the river to see what they might find. Lewis and Clark were trained military officers under orders directly from the president of the United States. In a letter likely written with a quill pen dated June 20, 1803, Thomas Jefferson gave explicit instructions, including:

> The object of your mission is to explore the Missouri River, and such principal streams of it, as, by its course and communication with the waters of the Pacific Ocean, whether the Columbia, Oregon, Colorado, or any other river, may offer the most direct and practicable water-communication across the continent, for the purposes of commerce.
>
> Beginning at the mouth of the Missouri, you will take observations of latitude and longitude, at all remarkable points on the river, and especially at the mouths of rivers, at rapids, at islands, and other places and objects distinguished by such natural marks and characters, of

a durable kind, as that they may with certainty be recognized hereafter. The courses of the river between these points of observation may be supplied by the compass, the log-line, and by time, corrected by the observations themselves. The variations of the needle, too, in different places, should be noticed.

Your observations are to be taken with great pains and accuracy; to be entered distinctly and intelligibly for others as well as yourself; to comprehend all the elements necessary, with the aid of the usual tales, to fix the latitude and longitude of the places at which they were taken; and are to be rendered to the war-office, for the purpose of having the calculations made concurrently by proper persons within the United States. Several copies of these, as well as of your other notes, shoed be made at leisure times, and put into the care of the most trust worthy of your attendants to guard, by multiplying them against the accidental losses to which they will be exposed. A further guard would be, that one of these copies be on the cuticular membranes of the paper-birch, as less liable to injury from damp than common paper.

Note that President Jefferson did not share our fixation with correct or even consistent spelling. Yet in a few concise pages he communicated clearly the information that current methods of government correspondence would likely require a document of the size of the New York phone book to accomplish.

Lewis and Clark took these orders very seriously. They took with them several compasses, including a surveyor's compass with spare needles and a magnet to "polarize" them, telescopes, a sextant, spirit and telescopic levels, a "Hadley's quadrant" or octant, rods and chains, artificial horizons, drafting instruments, a measuring tape, and a chronometer. They had an ephemeris, a book with tables giving the daily locations of sun, moon, and planets for use in celestial navigation. Unlike Columbus they could determine where they were, and they did so as part of their daily routine. They were thus able to make maps of remarkable accuracy for the day, to divide and rejoin the Corps, and to make it home safely. They lost only one man. Sargent Floyd died, likely of a burst appendix, on the outward-bound leg of the trip. You can visit a monument at his grave high above the Missouri River in Sioux City, Iowa, 42° 28' 38.82" N latitude, 96' 22' 8.27" W longitude, UTM 14, 716267 E, 4706144 N. Lewis and Clark were reasonably proficient celestial navigators. Our sextant is on the shelf and our celestial skills have gone south with our memory of calculus, but as long as we can keep power in our GPS, we almost always know exactly where we are.

CHAPTER 5

➤ Using a GPS on the Road

You've packed your gear for a long-planned outing to a destination you've never visited and are ready to hit the road. There are many strategies for using your GPS unit to make the trip easier. What works best for you will depend on the capabilities of your GPS unit, the nature of your trip, and your personal navigation preferences. Some people want to know exactly where they are all the time. Others insist on waiting until they are thoroughly lost before they bother to figure out where they really are. Most of us are somewhere in between, although we will touch on both extremes. In this chapter, we'll discuss strategies for using your GPS on the first portion of your outdoor trip, which will likely be by car or truck.

GPS units are common in automobiles today, with large-format color screens that show you where your vehicle is and can give voice prompts to alert you to upcoming turns. Receivers from Garmin, Magellan, TomTom and others can be mounted on the dash and make automobile navigation easy. The disadvantage for the outdoorsman, of course, is their size and weight, making them impractical for taking on the trail. So the strategies we will discuss assume that once you've parked your vehicle, you'll be taking the same GPS unit on the trail, or across the field—someplace beyond the vehicle. That means we will only touch on the use of personal digital assistants and notebook computers and focus on GPS units that can fit in your pocket, preferably in one piece.

SAVE THE GPS UNTIL YOU NEED IT?

We find GPS receivers very useful tools, some of the time. There are occasions where the effort simply does not yield real benefits. We all see people with a cell phone stuck in their ear, babbling on meaninglessly. They follow one conversation with another like chain smokers, addicted to continuous contact--afraid to be alone. Then there are the PDA micromanagers, spending much of their day keeping track of every event in the hope that it will somehow keep them organized and make them either more important or more money. We see GPS junkies as well, using the device to verify the location of every road sign, setting as many waypoints as their unit can handle. When traveling legs of your trip that are on well-marked roads, particularly the interstate highway system, you may want to leave the unit turned off. Save the distraction and enjoy the conversation and view. If you are on a long trip, you may want to turn it on occasionally to let it update. Otherwise it may take several minutes to initialize when you finally do turn it on.

USING GPS IN A VEHICLE

You've initialized and set up your GPS unit with the correct time and units, then matched the datum with the map you will be using. When you use it in a vehicle, there are several concerns that need to be addressed. The first is safety. A GPS unit can be an even bigger distraction than a cell phone. If you're driving a vehicle, you should be very cautious in attempting to check your position while in motion. Some larger map display units are designed for dashboard mounting specifically so you *can* see them while driving. Simpler units without maps—particularly older units with smaller, low-resolution screens—require considerable visual focus and mental concentration. Don't look at anything that takes your eyes completely off the road unless you have pulled off at a safe location and stopped.

A second concern is reception. Unless you are driving a convertible with the top down, your vehicle is a pretty effective antenna shield. You may get adequate reception by placing the unit on the dash, but as soon as you pick it up and move it away from the windshield, the accuracy of the unit will start degrading. All major GPS manufacturers produce small auxiliary antennae. If your GPS unit can connect to one, and if you want good reception in a vehicle, get one. The antenna can lie forward on the dashboard or be stuck low on the windshield with a suction cup bracket.

A third concern is power—in other words, battery drain. If you are using the GPS only for an occasional position check, this is not much of an issue. If you are on an all-too-typical long road trip to really "get away from it all" and plan to have the unit on continuously, however, it's almost inevitable that you will eventually hear the low-power alarm or, worse yet, pick up the unit and find a blank screen. Most units can operate on 12-volt power from your cigarette lighter adapter using an auxiliary cable. We highly recommend you get one, and use it.

An auxiliary antenna can significantly improve reception. Tape them to the top of your hat on the trail.

Still another issue is connecting your GPS to other display devices. A handheld GPS receiver can be connected to a PDA or notebook computer equipped with mapping software. We discuss this in greater detail elsewhere, but note that this will require yet another specialized cable. Some manufacturers offer a dual DC power and serial data cable.

Finally, think about maps. A typical American state road map has a scale of 1:500,000. Most road atlases are even smaller. Some may have small latitude and longitude tick marks along the edge, but many do not. Almost none have UTM grid markings. If your GPS unit displays maps or if you are linking it to a PDA or notebook that does, standard road maps or an atlas should be sufficient for on-road travel. If, however, you are using a nonmap GPS, get a better map—preferably one that's no larger in scale than 1:250,000, and with the UTM grid extending all the way across, not just ticks at the edge.

If you prefer not to travel with a number of large maps that are often difficult to roll out and view in a vehicle, state atlases are a good alternative. About the same size as a standard highway atlas, these publications typically cover only one state. DeLorme publishes an impressive series of Atlas and Gazeteers for all fifty states. Colorado is shown at a combination of 1:160,000 and 1:320,000, while Kansas is 1:200,000. Regrettably, many of these provide latitude and longitude tick marks only in the margins, meaning you will need to spend a lot of time drawing lines to make them useful. Newer versions for some states do have a grid at 10' or smaller intervals, although it is often difficult to distinguish from other lines. Benchmark Maps publishes very elegant atlases for many western states with an easy-to-read grid at 15' intervals. The New Mexico one we've used was at a scale of 1:525,000, making it somewhat small in scale for GPS use, even on the road. None we've seen has a UTM grid, but map publishing is a robust competitive business, and given the rapid expansion of GPS use someone is bound to seize the

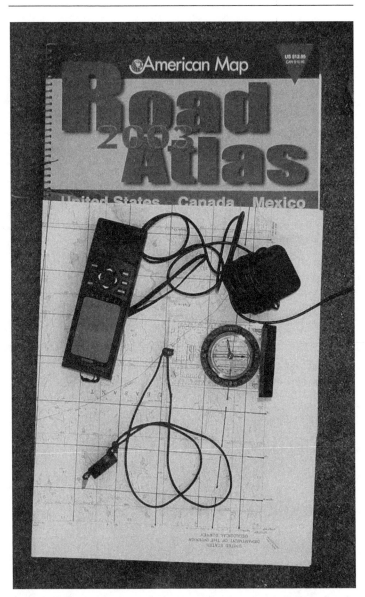

A GPS unit can be a useful navigation tool on the road and off. If you are really headed for the boonies, don't forget a good map and compass.

opportunity, hopefully soon. (Delorme's topo software does include a UTM grid.)

We'll work through a series of GPS-aided trips, starting with a simple GPS receiver, common large-scale maps, and very basic navigation strategies. This approach works just fine for many trips. Incrementally we will add the use of more detailed maps, more sophisticated GPS receivers, digital maps, and more precise navigation in more complex settings. There are many strategies that can be used for effective use of a GPS on the road. The seven we will discuss are:

1. Simply determining location with a basic GPS.
2. Manually entering waypoints in a basic GPS, creating a route, and following it.
3. Planning a route on a paper map and following it on a map-capable GPS unit.
4. Planning a route with map software on your computer, downloading it to a map-capable GPS, and following it to your destination.
5. Selecting a destination on a map-capable GPS and using its GOTO autorouting feature to take you there.
6. Connecting your GPS to a PDA equipped with a Pocket PC mapping program, then using the autorouting feature with voice commands to direct you to the location.
7. Connecting your GPS to a PC equipped with a Windows mapping program, with or without autorouting, and following your location on screen.

DETERMINING LOCATION

During the on-road portion of many outdoor trips, a GPS unit is used to find or verify your location when the road signs get a little iffy. It's convenient, but not absolutely essential, to have the route marked on your paper maps—and electronic maps, if your GPS unit displays them or you are using a PDA or notebook. Turn the unit on and place it where it can see enough satellites to get a fix. Again, it's a good idea to make sure the unit is set to the same datum as your map, although an error of a few hundred meters is not a real concern if you are trying to figure out which county you are in. When the GPS unit gets a position fix, note the grid location and mark it on the map. We often note the time as well on the paper map.

MANUALLY ENTERING WAYPOINTS IN A BASIC GPS

Upland bird season is still a few weeks away, and we need to work the dogs to get them ready. We're headed from Lawrence, Kansas, to the Barrel Springs Hunt Club, a licensed shooting preserve near Tribune in far western

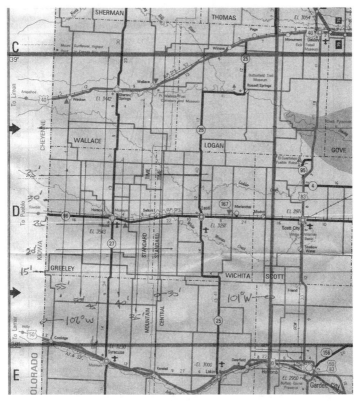

Map of the region around Tribune, Kansas.

Kansas. We'll be arriving at night in a flat, featureless land-scape where, as the old saying goes, "It's not the end of the world, but you can see it from here." The map from the Web site (http://www.barrelsprings hunt.com/) gives us a general idea of where to go.

Looking in the glove box of the truck, we then find a "1995–96 Official Kansas Transportation Map" that will probably be enough to get us there. Still, maybe we can use it with the basic GPS receiver we picked up at the new sporting goods store's grand opening for just over $ 100 to make the trip more convenient.

The map has only a graphic scale indicating about 12 miles per inch, or about 1:750,000. There are no UTM markings, but latitude and longitude ticks are marked by degree around the perimeter.

Using a moderate-width red marker, we extend latitude lines across the map and longitude lines up and down the map, creating a grid. A 5' grid is created around Tribune using a finer red line. Our destination is at 101° 44'W 38° 28'N, more or less. Our route will take us west on 1-70 from Lawrence to Oakley, through Topeka, Junction City, Salina, and Hays. We'll exit 1-70 in the dark and head west-south-west on US 40. At Sharon Springs, we'll head south on KS 27 to KS 96 in Tribune. West 2 miles, then north, and look for the sign on the north side of the railroad tracks.

The Garmin eTrex is a basic GPS unit lacking maps, but it is still a powerful nagivation tool. Courtesy: Garmin.

It's hard to get lost on I-70, and we could reasonably set the GPS aside until we reach

Oakley, but building a route that includes intermediate way-points marked by exits at larger cities will provide useful information. We can draw a 5' grid around each exit as we did for the Tribune area or, lacking more detailed maps, we could find the information online at the longitude/latitude position-finder site—http://www.juggling.org/bin/un.cgi/map-find.

WAYPOINTS: LAWRENCE TO THE BARREL SPRINGS HUNT CLUB WEST OF TRIBUNE

CITY	WAYPOINT	LATITUDE	LONGITUDE
Lawrence	LAWTP	39° 59' N	95° 15' W
South Topeka	STOPTP	39° 00' N	95° 42' W
West Topeka	WTOP70	39° 03' N	95° 47' W
I-70/KS 177 Junction	I70177	39° 04' N	96° 32' W
Junction City	JUNCO	39° 00' N	95° 50' W
Abilene	ABILEN	38° 56' N	97° 13' W
Salina	SALINA	38° 52' N	97° 38' W
Hays	HAYS	38° 54' N	99° 19' W
Oakley	OAKLEY	39° 07' N	100° 48' W
Sharon Springs	SHSPGS	38° 54' N	101° 45' W
Tribune	TRIBUN	38° 28' N	101° 45' W
Horace	HORACE	38° 28' N	101° 47' W
Barrel Springs	BSPGS	38° 28' N	101° 42' W

Compared to entry-level GPS receivers of a few years ago, the basic eTrex is an impressive unit. There are other eTrex models with more features. It has no built-in memory, and therefore no maps. You can set up only one route at a time, but it does offer 12-channel reception, up to 500 waypoints, and up to 50 waypoints in a track. The four-level gray LCD screen shows only 128 by 64 pixels and measures a tiny 2.1 by 1.1 inches, but we have found that it provides acceptable viewability. The eTrex does offer trackback capability, allowing you to retrace your path. It weighs only 5.3 ounces and has a 17-hour battery life on a couple of AA's. It interfaces well with map software running on a notebook computer. It also sports a high-sensitivity receiver, making it better able to find satellites even under dense cover, a significant problem in GPS receivers lacking this feature.

To use it on this trip, we will enter the waypoints listed above and string them together to form a route that we will then follow. We will be traveling major marked roads and will not be bothering with electronic maps. The eTrex will be used to keep us from making fundamental navigation errors, such as getting significantly off route. The eTrex is weather sealed and has only five buttons—power, page, enter, and a pair of up-down toggle buttons—but the data entry sequence is refined, if a bit tedious. If you are doing this in-

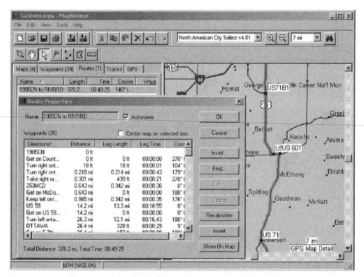

Connect waypoints to create a route. Set your typical speeds by type of highway in the EDIT PREFERENCES dialog. The software calculates the length and travel time of each leg, allowing you to evaluate the time consequences of alternative routes.

doors, the eTrex will tire of looking for satellites and display a screen asking *are you indoors now?* Clicking *enter* on the *yes* tab allows you to proceed with setup, and waypoint and track entry. The *waypoint* screen, accessible from the main menu, creates a default name and location based on its current or last-known position. Toggle up or down to the item you want to edit, click *enter,* and an edit screen specific to each item will appear. Use the toggle to move to the space you want to fill and click *enter,* and an alphabet selection box appears. Use the toggle to scroll through the alphabet and select the letter or number you want. Waypoint names are limited to six characters. If you get somewhere you don't want to be, clicking on the *page* button will usually back you out of it. Edit the screen to get the correct longitute, latitude, and (if you plan to use it) elevation of each waypoint. We enhanced our accuracy a bit by finding more precise values in a mapping software program. You can also find this information online, but estimating it from the map graphically will still help you detect serious navigational mistakes—you may just be a bit farther down the road before you know about them.

Keying in a dozen waypoints takes a few minutes and can leave you with sore fingertips. There is some advantage to starting the names on a particular trip with the same first letter, making them easier to assemble into a route. But since you can store up to 500 waypoints, you should consider entering points that may be used frequently, such as major intersections you often use, with obvious names and more precise coordinate information.

After entering all waypoints, go back to the main menu screen and select *route.* The eTrex will display an index of all your way-points. Toggle to the section of the alphabet where your first waypoint is, click *enter,* scroll to the waypoint, and click *enter* to add it to your route. The *route* screen will be displayed; by toggling to the blank waypoint at the bottom of the screen and clicking on it, you can enter the next waypoint. Continue this process until all waypoints have been entered into your route.

You can only store one route, so when you are ready to begin your trip, activate the eTrex, go to the main menu, toggle to the *route* tab, and click on *enter* to bring up the route you stored earlier. Toggle to the bottom of the screen and click on *follow*. You may need to place the GPS farther forward on the dash or even get out of the vehicle to acquire a fix. As soon as the GPS has been able to acquire enough satellite information for a position fix, a compass heading, or pointer page, a screen will appear. At the top of the screen is the name of the next way-point in your route, the straight-line distance to it, and the time to go as a function of speed. The top of the compass ring is the current direction of travel, and the large center arrow points in the direction you should travel to arrive at the next waypoint, indicated by the icon. You can select from an extensive list of icons when you originally enter each waypoint.

Using the *page* key, you can move to the *route* screen and scroll down to check the total distance to each waypoint. These distances are the cumulative direct line of travel between way-points. As we pass each waypoint, the eTrex jumps to the next, again indicating direct-line distance, course to waypoint, course to destination, and current speed. Depending on how far apart you set your waypoints and how many curves and bends there are in the road, the big course arrow will move left or right of your direction of travel, indicated by the vertical bar at the top of the compass ring. Seeing the big course arrow consistently pointing significantly left or right, or noting an unchanging or increasing distance to the next waypoint is a clear warning that you are likely off course. If that occurs, you have several options. Page to the *map* screen and you will get a very simplified diagram of your route. You can zoom in and out using the toggle buttons. The map will show waypoint names with a line connecting them, a north arrow (settable), and an icon showing your position and direction of travel. If you are left or right of track, you now know which direction you need to travel to get back on track. It's also time to start checking highway signs. If that is unfeasible, use the *page* key to get to the position page, find the coordinates of your position, and locate your position on the map. Don't attempt to do this while driving.

Located deep in the heart of the vast high plains of western Kansas, the Barrel Springs Hunt Club offers all the amenities expected in a premier hunt club. Guides direct hunters through more than 2,000 acres of prime pheasant habitat. It was definitely worth the trip.

The eTrex is a basic GPS, but we have revealed only a portion of its capability in this example of how to take advantage of it. The best way to learn how to use a GPS is to get outdoors and use it. Use it when you don't need to, when you know where you are going. Then, when you need it, you'll know how.

USING A GPS BASE MAP TO GO EXACTLY WHERE YOU PLAN

Many of us are most comfortable using a paper map—either a road atlas or a state highway map. This approach uses the GPS to determine position on the on-screen base map to follow a route planned on such a paper map. Mark your route with a color highlighter on a paper map, either the traditional type or one printed from map software or identified on Google Maps. If you're a thorough person, use software like Street Atlas and sites like www.randmcnally.com to avoid routes with excessive construction delays. When you head for the highway, activate your GPS receiver and its internal base map. Remember to keep the unit's antennae in a location where reception is not obstructed, and to exercise basic safety practices. This often means pulling off the road or putting a passenger in charge of navigation. The on-screen GPS map will display an icon showing your location; you can typically zoom in and out to get a better understanding of this site. The GPS unit provides a real-time indication of your location, along with your direction and speed of travel, making navigation using the paper map much more accurate.

DOWNLOADING DETAILED MAPS FROM A COMPUTER MAP PROGRAM

This approach uses the GPS unit as a guidance system. It suits several situations:

1. The persistently well-organized outdoor traveler.
2. A complicated trip through unfamiliar territory.
3. The need to provide others with detailed trip information.

Start by plotting and marking a detailed course on screen with map software that is compatible with the GPS unit you will be using on the trip.

All major GPS receiver manufacturers sell proprietary mapping software that works only with their units, and only with particular models. This software runs on a personal computer, either a desktop or notebook model. Some software packages cover an entire country, while others cover only certain states or provinces. Just how large an area you can transfer from the PC to the GPS unit depends on map detail, file size, and the amount of memory in your GPS unit. There has been a great deal of progress in compressing map files, but they still take a lot of memory. Add things like databases showing everything from gas stations to fishing hot spots and the files get even larger. Depending on the software and the GPS unit, you can:

> Create waypoints and routes on the computer and transfer them to the GPS unit for use with its built-in base map, or transfer a route created on the GPS or a recorded track for viewing or editing on the computer.
> Along with waypoint and route information, transfer detailed street and highway maps of the area you will be traveling through.

> Add detailed trail and topographic maps of the area you will be hiking or riding through.

Downloading maps with routes created on a computer works great, but if you do not have the software or the time, there are alternatives. Many GPS units incorporate autorouting software. We were skeptical about this feature at first, but with a little practice on how to select an address we were quickly impressed. Using the keys on the receiver we select a destination on a map-capable GPS and use its *goto* autorouting feature to take us there, connect our GPS to a PDA equipped with a Pocket PC mapping program, and use the autorouting feature with voice commands to direct us to the location. This makes the handheld the equivalent of the automobile GPS receivers commonly available today.

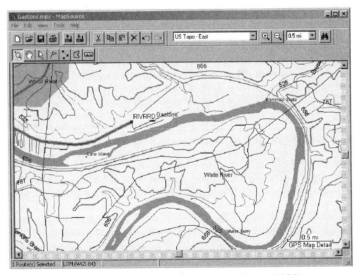

Garmin's MapSource TOPO provides detail comparable to USGS's great 1:100,000 maps. Shown here the tailwaters of the White River below Bull Shoals Dam in north-central Arkansas. You can download these to your GPS, and print maps of the areas you will be visiting.

LETTING THE GPS FIND YOUR LOCATION

Today's more sophisticated consumer-level GPS units have surprisingly accurate autorouting capabilities. This feature works with the base map that has major roads for the entire country, but it's significantly enhanced with the more detailed regional maps that you must select and download to the GPS from a PC. We have found the Garmin GPSMAP 76CSx with Garmin's Map Source Citi Navigator software a great tool for road navigation down to the county-road level. With and SD card with 128 MB of memory the unit can hold maps and extensive other data for eastern Kansas and western Missouri (expect less in more urban areas). File size appears to be increased by the extensive address and points-of-interest information.

We don't intend to provide a mini user's manual for this unit, but do want to show how the autorouting feature, now available on many GPS units, can be a powerful and convenient tool for on-road navigation in all but the most remote areas, provided they're equipped with good digital maps.

The menu systems on new GPS receivers clearly show the steady evolution of software logic and careful design of compact, higher-resolution, easy-to-read screens. The menu of the GPSMAP 76CSx offers distinct paths: *mark* a new waypoint, *find* a location, create or follow a defined *route,* start recording your movement as a *track, setup* the GPS, or use *accessories* that include a calculator, game, and a nifty moonrise/set and phase program, and others. *Find* offers clear options. The *addresses* option brings up a screen that asks for specific information. Toggle to the line you want to enter data in and hit *enter* to bring up the keypad. Similar screens are used extensively by this unit, tailored a bit for each type of data. With a little practice, data entry goes surprisingly fast, and the software brings up in the background the list of choices that match what you enter. As soon as you see what you are looking for, or think you are getting close, hit the *page* button, scroll down to the item you want to select, and press *enter.*

We have found the *find address* feature amazingly useful in larger urban areas, but the database has far less information on small-town and rural addresses. An easy solution is to use the *mark waypoint* feature and the *find waypoint,* or simply the *goto* option on the *mark waypoint* screen. The *mark waypoint* screen allows you to create a custom name, enter the location in the coordinate system that you set in the *setup* process, or search for your destination in the unit's map. When we first used this unit, we had real reservations about the prospect of finding a specific rural location on such a tiny screen, but have generally been favorably impressed. Searching for a new camping area within an hour's drive, for instance, we spotted the Old Military Trail Campground at a Corps of Engineers lake about 30 miles away and decided to check it out. We scrolled across the onscreen map, then zoomed in to the arm of the lake where the campground is located. The first few times we zoomed in on the wrong location, but with a few tries and a little scrolling we found our destination. After nudging the marking arrow to the campground entry trail, we pressed *enter* and marked the waypoint. The receiver responded with the coordinates of the marked point and, after changing the name, we hit the *goto* button. We got a query asking if we prefer to "Follow Road" or travel "Off Road." Choosing "Follow Road" brings up a message that the route is being calculated, and then the map appears with a magenta-colored line indicating the route on the map.

We placed the GPSMAP on the dash mount and, using the extension cord, put the antenna far forward on the dash. In a few seconds, it indicated it had reception on six satellites and a position fix with an accuracy of 18 feet, about the length of the vehicle. Paging to the autoroute-generated map, we immediately saw that it had charted a course that would take us through road construction we preferred to avoid. Instead of turning left, we turned right. The unit immediately picked up the turn and began recalculating a new route based on our direction of travel. This is a nifty feature, but one with idiosyncrasies. The program logic seems to require a minimum response time, so if you are rapidly approaching the next turn, it will route you in a loop to allow you more time to respond. We simply ignore it; as soon as we are on a straight stretch of road for a few blocks, it settles down and starts methodically taking us where we said we wanted to go. Depending on your speed and the type of road you are on, the unit will begin giving you turning instructions with an audible beep warning (unless you turned this off in *setup*) anywhere from a mile to a few hundred feet away, with incremental updates in screen detail and distance. You can also bring up a screen that lists all route turns in sequence, allowing you to preview the route for possible problems. The *trip information* page shows your current compass heading, speed, and other route information.

We arrived at our destination without difficulty, having been prompted at every turn. The one disappointment was the lack of warning as we approached our destination—the beep went off as we popped over a hill and overshot our des-

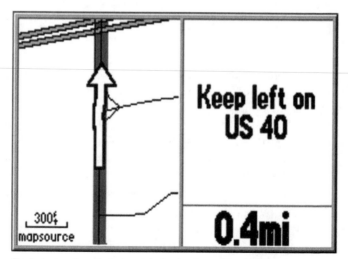

Route instructions include subtle instructions about highway layout.

tination. We turned around and turned down the lane into the campground, only to find it overgrown and locked—closed due to budget cuts.

We found the level of detail provided about lanes and intersections accurate and helpful. The location arrow always seems to be in the right location. Although the unit has good accuracy in most conditions, this is also a program feature: The arrow is placed on the road closest to the calculated position, unless that feature is turned off in *setup*.

The autoroute feature is a powerful tool. If you plan to use it, we encourage you to download detailed maps rather than relying on the less detailed base maps. Start by using it in familiar territory, too, so you can learn how it performs.

GPS WITH A PERSONAL DIGITAL ASSISTANT OR SMARTPHONE

Personal digital assistants, typically about 3 × 5 × ⅞ inches, weighing 4 to 6 ounces, and running on the Palm, Windows CE, or Windows Pocket PC operating systems, offer a unique opportunity for GPS. With screens typically 2½ × 2½ inches or larger, you can see maps in greater detail and greater area, and there is always that notion of a multifunctional device. The additional processor power, usually greater memory, and (with some units) ability to use Secure Digital (SD) or Compact Flash memory chips means you can store more maps and do more with them. Software packages are available that provide audible turning instructions that, combined with the not-too-small, not-too-big screen size, make a PDA easier and safer for many drivers. There are three basic strategies for using GPS with PDAs:

1. Direct integration.
2. A separate dedicated GPS connected by a cable, with all display handled by the PDA.
3. Connecting a fully functional stand-alone GPS to the PDA with a cable to gain additional screen size and processing power.

Direct Integration

PDAs with a Compact Flash slot, or a sleeve that provides one, can use GPS units designed to fit in CF slots. CF GPS receivers are available from several vendors. Putting everything in one unit like this seems logical; in actual use, however, by the time you get these integrated units far enough forward on the dash for good reception, the screens become difficult to view for some.

Nonscreen GPS Units Cabled to PDAs

GPS receivers without screens are available from several manufacturers, intended for connection to PDAs or notebook computers via cable or Bluetooth wireless technology. Many of these units require connection to a DC energy source to minimize energy drain from the PDA battery, making them unsuitable for trail use.

Maptech's Pocket Navigator provides routing and voice instruction capability.
Courtesy: Maptech

Stand-Alone GPS Units Cabled to PDAs

PDAs with mapping software installed, like MapTech's Pocket Navigator, provide great routing and voice instruction capability, although this may be more useful in urban settings than in getting to an outdoor destination. Conceptually, PDAs look like a great option for the outdoorsperson. They offer a larger map viewing area and more memory to store lots of detailed topo maps. They have one great bane— they are, relatively speaking, energy hogs. Without an AC or a DC adapter, these units drain their batteries in as little as an hour. Some units claim 8 to 10 hours. A few PDAs offer interchangeable batteries, but many do not. Every time more efficient processors offer the potential for lower power consumption and longer battery life, it seems to be taken back by the energy demand of fancier displays. You could lug one of those battery packs made up of multiple D cells down the trail to get a typical PDA battery life approaching that of a typical GPS unit. If your trip afield exceeds the PDA's battery life, however, the best approach—at least for now—is to leave the PDA in the vehicle and rely on a full-function GPS.

GPS WITH A NOTEBOOK PC

For real navigational power on the road, connect your GPS to a notebook PC running one of many good mapping software packages. More screen area (in color) and lots more processor power running sophisticated map software gives you access to all kinds of information. We've seen a few folks, usually in big cab pickups, mount a notebook in a bracket near the dash where they can view it while driving. Unless you've entered a route and set the PC to give you turning instructions so you can keep your eyes on the road, a passenger is really essential for safe travel using a PC. A configuration we typically use includes the following:

> A notebook PC with a CD drive and a spare serial port (to connect the GPS) with mapping software installed and

map CDs (we like DeLorme's Street Atlas, Topo USA, and state-specific 3-D TopoQuads).

➤ A GPS capable of connecting to the PC via a serial port and the vehicle's DC power system, preferably with a separate antenna. This provides better reception and keeps a potentially dangerous object off the dash. (No, we are not part of the scared-of-everything crowd, but we have learned firsthand where an object on the dash goes in a collision.)

➤ A multiplug DC adapter.

➤ A small (125-watt) inverter to connect the PC to the vehicle's DC power system.

➤ Cables for everything, and elastic bands to minimize the jungle they quickly create.

Connect the GPS to the PC, plug in its DC power connection, and place the antenna on the dash (use a suction cup mount or tape it down). Get the antenna as far forward as reasonably possible to improve reception. Turn on the GPS, then boot the PC. Place the CD with the maps you plan to use in the drive and load the map software. Hit the activate GPS icon and an onscreen graphic, typically an arrow, indicates your position. As your vehicle begins to move, the indicator scrolls across the map, showing your path of movement. Additional on-screen information includes course direction, speed (more accurately than your in-dash instrument), location, and altitude.

A word of caution. The first time or two getting this all to work may try your patience. Combine two electronic devices and a new Murphy is often born on the spot. Make sure the comm or USB port you are using is free on the PC. If, like many notebook users, you often attach an external mouse to the serial port, you will likely need to uninstall it. Make sure the GPS and PC are set for the same interface and baud rate, and that the GPS and map software are set to the same datum.

CHAPTER 6

> ## Using a GPS
> ## in the Field

Now you've arrived at the real starting point of your outdoor adventure. As you leave your vehicle and set out on foot or bike, you generally won't have roads and highway signs to help you find your way. Your GPS receiver now becomes a more important piece of gear. In this chapter we'll discuss how to use your GPS in the field. In addition to your receiver, don't forget a suitable map (properly prepared), a magnetic compass, and spare batteries.

Each of us is prone to adopt a method of navigation that suits our temperament, varying it with the complexity of the trip and our knowledge of the area. Some of us depart with a general notion of where we are going and wait until we are essentially lost to try to figure out where we are. This is not your typical American (male) outdoorsman, of course, but there are a few of us left. Others plan ahead in such detail that the process of navigation dominates the entire adventure. Actually, both extremes—and all the methods in between—can meet the requirements of a particular outing.

Most GPS receiver manufacturers publish user manuals ranging from good to excellent. Along with instructional videos, Web sites, and other available books, you should have no trouble learning how your particular unit operates, provided you invest the time and effort. Repeating this material would be of little value, particularly since each unit has some unique features and display sequences. Surprisingly, a lot of folks who have purchased a GPS receiver and learned the basics of its operation have not really figured out how to make it useful. Like a battery-operated nose hair clipper, it ends up at the bottom of the desk drawer—and when you finally decide to give it another shot, the batteries are dead. Let's hit the trail and look at a series of fairly typical outings, ranging from a day hike to a high-adventure backpacking trip, and consider how sensible use of a GPS receiver could make each trip safer and more fun. We'll start using basic GPS receivers without built-in maps and move on to map-equipped units.

Magellan's Crossover GPS is designed for use in a vehicle and then on the trail. Courtesy: Magellan.

FINDING YOUR LOCATION

It's late June and the snow should be off the high trails to a remote lake with an abundant population of cutthroats that seldom see an artificial fly, thanks to the 9-mile hike and 3,000-foot rise from the nearest access point. You've packed your fishing gear and are headed up the trail in the crisp morning air before the sun breaks over the peaks. It'll be easy to find; you were there 20-some years ago. A few thousand strides and the trail branches, but there's a sign making navigation easy. No need to check the map. Soon the sun is eclipsed by uncommon morning clouds and you enter a zone where a recent fire has ravaged the forest, and the trail. Distracted by the ghostly appearance of the scorched but standing pines, you plod on, now making sharp turns in long, steep switchbacks. Slowly it begins to dawn on you that you have no real sense of where you are or if you're actually headed in the right direction. Speaking of direction, that internal compass that always—well, almost always—keeps you from getting lost has inexplicably turned off. No sun, tall trees, steep rock bluffs, and the only directions you know for sure are up and down. You're pretty sure you could still backtrack. Maybe you should. It might rain. But there are none of those big beautiful cutthroats in that direction. You're sorely tempted to just keep moving, keep gaining elevation—surely *it will begin to grow familiar*—*but* you are also anxious to wet a line. When you come to an opening in the trees, you finally do it—get out the map and GPS unit and begin to figure out where you really are.

Now, of course this has never happened to us—it's strictly hypothetical—but if it, or anything remotely similar, ever happens to you, finding your location should be relatively easy. Hopefully you've remembered to:

1. Extend the UTM grid across your map in appropriate increments, if it didn't come with preprinted grids.
2. Set the GPS data to display coordinates in the UTM grid.
3. Set the GPS datum to match the map datum.
4. Initialize the GPS within a reasonable distance to minimize search time.
5. Find an open area away from dense woods and sheer rocks that could block the antenna.

Power up the GPS receiver. After the greeting screen, the *satellite status* page should appear. The screen format will vary depending on manufacturer and model, but the basic information is the same:

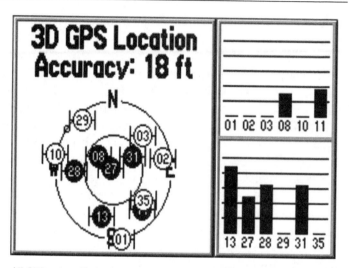

All GPS units will give you some indication of where the satellites are, which ones they have been able to acquire, and an indication of accuracy.

- A sky-view indication of the location of the satellites that should be "visible" to the receiver, often diagrammatically.
- An indication of individual satellites from which data has been received, often graphically.
- The signal strength of each satellite, and whether the unit has collected data required to help calculate a position fix.

While you are waiting for the GPS unit to acquire a position fix, you can use your magnetic compass to orient the map so that its north side is pointing north. Turn the rotatable dial until the north arrow is up. Place the compass on the map's magnetic north line and rotate the map and compass until the magnetic north needle aligns with the magnetic north line of the map. All GPS units will indicate direction when moving, but this feature does not work when you stop. There are a few units available that do have a built-in compass that works while you are standing still.

Watch the *status* page. Remember that the GPS unit needs to receive data from at least three satellites to compute a fix; more will reduce estimated position error. If the receiver is not acquiring data from enough satellites for a fix, take a look at your surroundings and try to move to a less obstructed location. Remember, your body can also block reception.

There are occasions when the process of acquiring a "quick" location fix turns into a trip-disrupting, time-consuming affair, payback for having been careless or cocky. But assuming we don't encounter such a problem, within a short time, typically two or three minutes, the GPS unit will calculate a position and jump to the *position* page.

The *position* page will show your location in the grid coordinates to which the GPS unit is set; we recommend UTM. Depending on the unit, other information typically displayed on this or the next page or two includes:

> Track direction and speed over the ground.
> Trip distance traveled.
> Elevation.
> Time.

Note the UTM coordinates and remember the saying, "Read right up." The first number is the false casting. If your position is on the map you are holding, it tells you how far right (east) you are from the left side of the map. The second number is the northing, telling you how far up from the bottom of the map your position is.

Great, we're not lost anymore! Well, we were never really lost, were we? Just not exactly sure how to get where we wanted to go as quickly as possible. We'd have made it eventually—right? We are on the wrong trail and about 60 degrees off course, but a quick look around at some prominent landmarks to reset the old compass between the ears, a fast 200-yard bushwhack downhill, and we'll be right on track. No need to waste batteries, so let's turn this handy gadget off and get on down the trail. We'll come out the same way we went in. In the dark.

RECORDING A TRACK AND RETRACING IT

You've hunted deer for decades, not for trophies, but for meat. Oh, you've got that little six-point mounted, the first deer you ever shot, but you're normally after a tender tasty yearling doe of 100 pounds or so. This time, however, a convergence of events has distracted you. An old friend has begun chiding you about the puny rack on your den wall, even comparing it to the size of, well, other things, and you've found a new place to hunt—one with several very large bucks. Not that they are going to get you into the record book, but one of them on the wall will put an end to any more disparaging remarks about your deer hunting skills. Besides, you need a challenge, and a reason for a better, or at least different, gun. Maybe a new bow, as well—one of those single-cam jobs.

Large bucks don't get that way being stupid, and except under the hormone-driven spell of the annual rut, the big ones are seldom seen in daylight. You've spent most September and October weekends carefully scouting your new hunting area. You understand their rubs, scrapes, and trails fairly well, and as the season approaches you know exactly what tree you want to be in at least an hour before the legal shooting time of 30 minutes before sunrise. That makes tree time about 5:30 A.M. The problem is getting there. Your deer tree is about a mile from where you will park, through diverse terrain, with patches of heavy brush, several deep ravines, and some thick woods, and you need to navigate it quickly and quietly—in the dark. Not even moonlight this season.

This is, of course, strictly hypothetical. We've never had friends who kidded us like that, and if we ever did we'd just ignore them, but we *can* tell you how to use your GPS unit to find a particular tree—in the dark. The same basic method works for finding your camp, duck blind, fishing hole, trapline, cache—whatever, day or night. It does take quite a bit more work than the first example. But understand, deer are bigger than trout, and you don't have to throw most of them back to be respectable.

Plan your route carefully. Use paper or electronic topo maps, use aerial photographs, but most importantly use your field experience. Break the route into segments, preferably relatively straight sections. You'll obviously want to avoid terrain that would be difficult to traverse in the dark, but you should also avoid thick woods that would impair GPS reception. Keep in mind that even a good GPS will rarely tell you precisely where you are, so avoid a route where being a few yards off the track could be dangerous. Each segment of your route or track is a *leg,* with the beginning and end of the route, as well as the joints between legs, defined as *waypoints. You* may want to think about short, descriptive waypoint names that are easier to remember than simple numbers. When you want to find a particular waypoint, it's often easier to remember *bigelm* or *fence* than 03 or 19. There are several ways to create a track. One is to walk the route with your GPS on, marking each turning point and giving it a waypoint name. Set a waypoint about every 5 minutes, even if you have not changed directions. Then build a route by combining them. An easier method is to set the GPS to record a track. Most will allow you to set the distance or time interval between track recording points.

Set up the GPS for the trip in the dark the night before. Make certain you have fresh batteries because this will drain them. If it is cold use lithium batteries. Under *system setup,* adjust the screen light timer to suit your strategy. If you anticipate needing to follow the GPS continuously, set it to *always on.* Adjust screen brightness and contrast in the dark so you can just comfortably see the screen. The brighter the screen, the poorer your night vision will be. If you want to optimize your night vision, cover the screen with a layer of red acetate film. In the morning darkness, you will need to have one and preferably two hands free, so plan your gear accordingly with a sling for your gun or bow.

When you park and are ready to head down the trail, turn on the GPS and allow it to acquire a position fix. From the main menu select *track* and then the track you want to follow, in this case *deer stand*. Indicate that you want to retrace the track on *GPS trackback*, and that you want to go to the *end of the track*.

Navigation instructions will vary by GPS. Some units respond with a compass or *direction finder* screen. Your direction of travel is at the top of the screen; the long arrow points toward the next waypoint. If it is pointing left or right, you are not traveling directly to the waypoint. The center section of the long arrow will drift left or right if you are off track. Data windows on the screen provide the distance to the next waypoint, speed of travel, and other information that you can set.

You could determine the coordinates of each waypoint from the maps and key them into your GPS receiver manually. We'll do that on our next outing.

PLANNING A ROUTE AND USING A GPS TO FIND AND FOLLOW IT

You are the event planner for your mountain bike club, and you're sponsoring a fall weekend ride that will involve as many as 150 riders. Saturday's ride will cover about 50 miles over rugged trails, with the group meeting at a campground for the evening, supper, and maybe a keg or two of microbrew. Sunday's ride will be a bit longer, looping back to the starting point by different routes. To minimize congestion and maximize the outdoor experience, your planning committee has decided to divide the large group into five smaller ones of roughly 30 each. You'll all start and end at the same place each day but take different trail routes between. Every rider will be given a custom map showing key terrain features, all the trails, and his or her individual route. Unfortunately, the terrain is complex—mountains tend to be that way—the web of trails is extensive, and there is virtually no signage. Mass confusion seems pretty much inevitable since few of the riders are familiar with the area. Aside from the ribbing you know you'll get as stragglers ride into camp late, you really aren't looking forward to searching for lost riders in the dark. When you find them, they will at first be thankful, and then angry.

A Garmin eTrex Vista mounted on a bide handlebar. Courtesy: Garmin.

Recalling that about 15 of your hard-core riders have purchased GPS units with handlebar mounts, you decide to provide the UTM coordinates of waypoints spaced out every mile on each route. By assigning GPS-equipped riders to each group, one at the front, one in the middle, and one riding sweep, you hope to minimize confusion. You don't have time to ride all the routes and mark the waypoints on tracks as we did in the search for the deer stand tree, but there are a couple of easy ways to get the track information to all 15 GPS units.

Having acquired the most detailed software your GPS vendor provides (we use Garmin's *MapSource US TOPO*), install it, open it, and find the specific area of interest. You can do this all on screen, but we generally find it much easier to start with a good paper trail map that lets you see a large region, one that provides good detail of the trails you will be using. A scale of 1:50,000 or less works best. Mark each trail with a distinct color and think of an appropriate short name. You will likely need to zoom in until your computer screen only shows an area a few miles wide before the trails start to display.

- Find the trail head, click on the route tool, and click on the trail head location.
- The cursor will now drag a color line across the screen that represents a leg of your route, while the bar at the bottom of the screen shows the distance and bearing from the first mark at the trail head to the location of the cursor.
- Mark each subsequent waypoint along the entire trail route, scrolling across the screen as necessary. Be sure to place waypoints at key turns and at least every half mile, but don't place so many that you will exceed the capacity of the GPS units your riders will use (unlikely).
- The program will let you edit the Route name, and Waypoint names. Edit them to reflect actual geographic names in the area but keep them concise so as not to exceed the capability of the GPS units.
- You can now save the route file in the proprietary format of the vendor (mps for Garmin) or export it in text (txt) or graphic format (typically dxf).
- If everyone is using the same brand of GPS you can simply email them or hand them a CD with the files for transfer to their GPS via serial or USB cable from their computer. More likely there will be several brands of GPS units and they tend to like their proprietary formats. There are several shareware programs that translate route files between them. We like GARtrip, available at http://www.gartrip.de/, although you will need to pay a $35 fee to get a fully functional copy.

What if you don't have the rather pricey vendor specific map software? Get on the Web and go to http://www.easygps.com and download EasyGPS, a shareware program from TopoGrafix.

Easy GPS lets you create, edit, and transfer waypoints and routes between your computer and a Garmin, Magellan, or Lowrance GPS. Using EasyGPS, you can manage your waypoints and routes, and display them in lists sorted by name, elevation, or distance. EasyGPS connects your GPS to the best mapping and information sites on the Internet, giving you one-click access to street and topo maps, aerial photos, even weather forecasts. Download the brief User's Manual, review it, and open the program.

➤ Right click on the screen and click on New Waypoint. Enter the approximate coordinates of the area your trail starts and give it a name.

➤ Right click on the line the waypoint data appears on and select View Waypoint Online and your Web Browser will open the EasyGPS Waypoint Viewer page giving you choices of a number of sources for viewing maps on line or ordering paper or electronic maps. Each has their merits, but click on Microsoft TerraServer under Topo Maps.

➤ Navigate to the map of your area with one of the options provided—place name often works well.

➤ Pan to the specific area of the specific trails you are looking for. Set the map resolution for maximum and map size for large. Click the Info tab on the top bar and longitude and latitude values, as well as UTM values will appear next to the grid. Adjust your browser screen size so you can read off the grid values accurately using a ruler or scale and transfer them to the EasyGPS screen.

As you complete all the waypoints for the route for each trail you can save the file in one of two formats, a TopoGrafix Data File (*.loc) or GPS Exchange File (*.gpx). You can send the loc file to all GPS equipped participant. They can download the free EasyGPS program, configure it for the GPS unit, open the loc file, and transfer it via cable to their GPS unit.

GPX lets you exchange data with other GPS users, who might not be using the same software as you. Check it out at http://www.topografix.com/gpx_for_users.asp.

AN EXPEDITION: ENJOYING TWO WEEKS ON THE TRAIL IN THE HIGH COUNTRY

As a dedicated practitioner of outdoor sports, from big-game hunting to bird-watching or bike riding, you understand that in a world with more than six billion people, many of them scraping to survive or pillaging to get rich, the future of what we cherish requires stewardship on a global scale. Responsible stewardship of our natural world requires that we have some understanding of its diversity, its complexity, and its limits for tolerating abuse. Having realized long ago that there is no hope of teaching this to executives of large corporations or more than a tiny handful of politicians, you have targeted your public service commitment to teaching members of a youth group (scouts, church, what have you) how to enjoy and appreciate the great outdoors. Hopefully their generation will do better than we have.

During the past three years, the members of your youth group have been active and had a lot of fun honing their outdoor skills locally. They are capable campers, several are budding naturalists, and they all have a greater appreciation of the outdoor world. All this has whet their appetites to go where they have never gone before. They want an adventure. A high adventure. Brainstorming, Web browsing, and calls to rangers at various agencies finally identify a unique area of the Rockies that sees little summer hiking pressure. It just takes a lot of work to get there. The 25 youths and eight adults will be divided into four crews that will hike separate routes over a two-week period, each covering more than 100 miles. None of you has undertaken a trip of this scale before, and none of you has ever visited the area. Your assignment is to lead the effort to find adequate maps, plan specific routes, and make sure they minimize the risk of getting lost.

Aside from the potential danger involved, getting lost is simply not fun. It puts a damper on the trip, and memories of the trip, and it creates embarrassment you will never live down. We know some teenage boys who twenty years from now will still be laughing at their scout leader who had them lost in the Rockies for two days. This is not hypothetical, but it wasn't us.

This is a big undertaking and those responsible are assuming a great deal of responsibility. Start planning early. Failure to plan is to plan to fail. If you think you can do it in three months, allow six. Some folks may think you are anal, but a smooth fun trip will cure them.

> Get good maps of the area you plan to visit, paper for certain, and software if at all possible. Many sources are mentioned in this book and the ever changing Web can help you find more. Study them carefully, identifying trails, major features, and campgrounds. Think about where you will get water. Analyze the terrain and start thinking about how much distance you realistically can and want to cover each day.

> Do research. Read travel guides, visit web sites, call park rangers and talk to them, most are eager to help. Learn about use restrictions and camp site reservation policies. Describe what you are considering doing in detail and get their advice.

> Start meeting with the entire group to organize your crews, select crew leaders, and crew navigators. Consider appointing two, one using only a compass, the other compass and GPS, and rotate their roles. A little friendly competition improves performance. Make sure they have their equipment and know both its limitations and how to use it. Have them make sure they understand the map's grid, enhancing them if necessary. Practice finding a GPS grid position on the map.

➤ Carefully plan each day's travel out and back. Plan to go slow at first while you are acclimating to the thinner mountain air.

➤ A layover day with a side trip is also a good idea. Mark the route on the map with a waterproof marker and fold it for storage in a waterproof map case. Duplicate maps are a good idea.

➤ Prepare a trip description with the grid location, altitude, and name of the waypoints for each major leg of the trip. At a minimum it should include each night's camp. Major landmarks, and significant course changes are also very helpful. Leave a copy behind at home and with someone at the trail-head when you go, and let them know when you return.

➤ Using any of the methods described above, enter the route in at least one GPS. Entering each day as a separate route works best, clearly labeling them.

➤ When the big day finally comes and you are at the trail head don't just start down the trail. Look around, orient the map, check the GPS position and reconcile it with the map. From map, compass and GPS, determine the course of the first leg. Open the saved route file on the GPS. Identify at least one and preferably two landmarks that can aid you in following the course without having to look at the compass or GPS too frequently. Do this at every major course change. Note the time on the map and go for it.

➤ Modern GPS units have many features that can help you navigate, but unless you take lots of batteries you are not going to have it on continuously to make use of many of them. Just remember, the way to not get lost is to continuously keep track of where you are. Whenever in doubt, check your position. Turn on the GPS and make certain the correct route file is active. As soon as it acquires a position fix it will show you how far off track you are. You can also transfer the position coordinates to the map to "get a bigger picture". If trees or cliffs are blocking reception you may need to seek a clearer area to determine where you are.

Throughout the planning process work on getting the crew in shape. Regardless of age or camping experience, trekking in the mountains with a heavy pack is hard work. Weekend shakedown hikes under pack of gradually increasing length and difficulty are important steps, along with regular exercise.

 # Geocaching

Geocaching is a relatively new sport. Geocaching is modern hobby treasure hunting. You're not supposed to actually keep the treasure, but trade for it, all on the honor system, and you'll need a GPS to play. Actually it's a lot of fun and provides a useful framework with which to hone your GPS navigation skills. If you felt you had to wait for hunting or fishing season to have an excuse to be outdoors, this game will expand your season.

Cache (pronounced *kash)* is a noun derived from the French verb *cacher,* meaning "to conceal." A *cache is* a place in which stores of food or supplies are hidden. *Caching is* to hide or store things in a cache, according to *Webster's.* The fundamentals of the game are simple.

Hide It

➤ Hide something, or a bunch of things. The one essential item is a logbook. You'll usually want to protect it from the weather. Use your imagination to make your treasure as easy or challenging to find as you choose. Hide some old interesting collectibles of little value, or hide something of significant value, but make it very difficult to find. One technique is to string caches, with one providing direction to another. The rules are constantly evolving and changing, so use your imagination. Urban caches can be particularly challenging. Don't hide spoilable food, drugs, guns, ammunition, or explosives, and remember this is a sport for all ages so potentially offensive items are not welcome.

> Record the precise location (waypoint) using your GPS unit. Note the datum and location in both lat/long and UTM.

> Post the location and information about the cache on one or more of several Internet geocaching sites.

> Check the cache occasionally and update the Web site(s), especially if it is removed.

Find It

> Visit one of the Web sites and identify caches near where you are or plan to go.

> Find the cache using your GPS unit. It will seldom be as easy as you think.

> Take something, but replace it with something of comparable interest or value.

> Don't move the cache unless instructed to do so. If you find a "Travel Bug" you are encouraged to help move it along, and to report it on the Web. Some items have made it around the world with surprising speed.

> Log your visit at the cache and on the Web.

> Serious bird-watchers keep a life book of bird sightings. Serious geocachers do the same.

A great place to start is http://www.geocaching.com. A few steps through their search engine yields a map and list of nearby caches.

Clicking on the one in the area we plan to visit yields further details. Note that I can download the waypoint and use EasyGPS to move it to my GPS unit. If I were seeking several caches, this would be helpful, but with only one I'll just key it in.

An accessory for the Garmin eTrex is a handlebar mounting bracket. After installing the bracket and clicking the GPS in place, we hit the River Levee Trail described in the geo-cache.com Web site.

After clicking on *find* in the GPS main menu screen, then *waypoint,* we selected GC83FD—the name we entered for the waypoint because that was the name used in the Web site. Pressing the *goto* button gets us a screen telling us to head east to a point 4.87 miles away. If we find it easier, we can set the screen for large fonts.

We head down the trail in search of the cache. We'll leave the rest to your imagination.

Many GPS units include capabilities tailored to geocaching. Courtesy: Garmin

GPS Units with Geocaching Capability

There are a number of GPS receivers on the market now whose features reflect the increased popularity of geo-caching. Some Garmin models, for example, feature a "Geo-cache" icon in their Find screen. Selecting this feature brings up a list of nearby geocaches in the unit's memory, getting there either manually by the user or downloaded from the internet. Navigate to the geocache and the unit's compass page switches to special geocaching mode, which displays information specific to the cache that may have been included with the internet download. Once found, the cache is recorded by the GPS with an entry in the unit's calendar, and the GPS displays an option to locate the next nearest cache.

Some Geocaching Web Sites
http://www.geocaching.com/

Buxley's Geocaching Waypoint
http://www.brillig.com/geocaching/

Navicache.com—A GPS Stash Hunt Website
http://www.navicache.com/

http://www.terracaching.com

http://geocacher-u.com
This "Geocacher University" site features a variety of articles about geocaching, mainly for those getting started.

CHAPTER 8

➤ Mapping and Related Software

Just when you begin to think using a GPS will make it easy to get where you want to go, you discover the extensive and fast-changing world of electronic maps, where it seems every player wants to do things a bit differently. Most GPS units are capable of displaying maps on their small screens. Display size limits the geographic area that can be viewed, but they are very helpful. Most units come with a "base map" of major highways and geographic features for the entire country already loaded. GPS manufacturers also offer the ability to download more detailed maps, by either cable or memory chip, and the ability to download and upload waypoint and route information. If you have the time and money, you can now download maps, even aerial photographs, via cell or satellite phone and view them, along with your GPS determined position, on a notebook or PDA. In this chapter we'll look at some of the features of electronic maps and map software. This is a rapidly changing field of which we will provide an overview, but by no means a comprehensive account of available products.

BASE MAPS

As mentioned above, most GPS units come with a "base map" of major highways and geographic features for the entire country. Such base maps typically consume relatively little memory and will get you down the interstate just fine. Fancier units have 24 to 64 MB of memory, or offer the option of an SD card with 128 MB of memory or more for the storage of more detailed maps of specific areas where you plan to travel. Most GPS manufacturers offer a variety of map CDs in proprietary format specific to their hardware. Third-party vendors offer mapping software that may be compatible with more than one GPS manufacturer. In all cases you must use a separate personal computer to run the software and prepare the map or maps for transfer to the GPS unit's memory. Map data transfer typically requires connecting the GPS to the computer via serial or USB cable, or placing the memory card in a separate card reader.

Bear in mind that the availability of detailed digital maps is limited for the more remote parts of the world, including North America. Creating digital maps is labor-intensive, and map makers with finite resources put their efforts into creating maps of areas that will likely be of interest to sizable numbers of people, thus increasing sales of the map. Therefore, detailed digital maps of more remote areas are not likely to show up as soon maps for more well traveled areas.

GPS memory may be fixed internally or on a removable card. Several manufacturers use proprietary removable memory cards. Others use common Compact Flash or Secure Digital cards, which are generally less expensive. When selecting a GPS receiver, consider carefully the map software that best suits the types of outdoor activities you plan to pursue.

When GPS units are connected to a personal digital assistant, notebook PC, or tablet PC the range of map software available expands significantly. These devices are capable of handling a wide range of mapping and geographic information software with such features as:

➤ Detailed location on large-scale, high-resolution maps and aerial photographs.

➤ Extensive map files eliminating the need for memory downloads for each trip or use of memory cards.

➤ Automatic routing (also available on some GPS receivers).

- Route optimization.
- Detailed guidance, including voice instructions.
- On-the-road access to maps, aerial photographs, weather, and other information via cell phones or wireless networks.
- Route profiles and 3-D views.
- Printer output of customized maps.

The real problem for the outdoorsman is that these devices are too large, too heavy, and too power hungry to be useful afield. We often find that the best option is use a separate GPS unit suitable for the trail, but to connect it to a PDA or notebook PC while on the road to permit access to more robust software. Still, GPS and computer hardware are both evolving at a rapid pace—and so is the software to support them. The single electronic device incorporating PDA, mobile phone, GPS, and other features is beginning to appear in the form of more sophisticated Smartphones.

ELECTRONIC MAPS FROM GPS MANUFACTURERS FOR GPS UNITS

Powerloc Technology, Destinator

Destinator is a GPS navigation system that includes a GPS receiver and mapping software based on NAVTECH maps, all configured for use with PDAs and Smartphones. The NAVTECH-based maps are highly compressed, permitting download of whole states from a PC to a flash card.

Features include:

- The ability to input your destination or select from an address list.
- Turn-by-turn voice prompts guiding you to your destination.
- Your option—shortest or quickest route.
- The ability to show dynamic and interactive maps.
- Automatic recalculation of alternate route if you miss a turn.

- Full-featured menus and audiovisual navigation.
- 26-language capacity.
- Storage for up to 4,000 destinations in the address book.
- Instant recall of the last 15 destinations.
- Complete portability—no installation required.
- Detailed street maps of the United States and Canada.

Garmin Mapsource

Garmin (http://www.garmin.com/cartography/) publishes an extensive set of electronic maps under the MapSource name. Included in the series are Marine, Fishing Hot Spots, BlueChart, City Navigator, City Select, MetroGuide, and TOPO. With MapSource software, you can view color maps on a personal computer, with zoom and pan functions that allow easy map browsing. The *trip* and *way-point manager* functions allow you to create waypoints, routes, and tracks, and transfer them from your PC by cable or a memory card to most Garmin GPS units. Some Garmin products require valid unlock codes for installation and use. Several of Garmin's MapSource programs of particular interest to the outdoorsman are discussed in greater detail below.

City Navigator provides extensive coverage of metro and rural areas throughout the contiguous United States and Canada. It includes information for highways, interstates, and business and residential streets, with turn restrictions, speed categories, and other navigation features. Features include:

- Trip and waypoint management functions.
- Local, county, and residential roads as well as interstates for all 50 states.
- Point-of-interest information (with nearly 6 million points) such as service stations, gas stations, restaurants, hotels, campsites, hospitals, banks, and more.

These functions of this product work with nearly all Garmin GPS units.

The **TOPO DVD** selection of MapSource contains digital topographic maps for the United States, including Alaska and Hawaii, that are comparable to the U.S. Geological Survey 1:100,000 scale paper maps. Features include:

> Trip and waypoint management functions.
> Highways, roads, hiking trails, snowmobile trails, backwoods trails, elevation contours, point elevations, summits, some bathymetric contours, geographic names, churches, and schools.
> Shoreline detail for lakes, reservoirs, small bodies of water, waterways, rivers, and streams.
> Icons representing boat ramps, dams, marinas, campgrounds, public facilities, mile markers, first-aid stations, wrecks, fuel, dangerous and restricted areas, and picnic, swimming, and ski areas.
> Nautical navaids for the 50 states including radiobeacons, RACONs, and fog signals; river, harbor, and other lights; and daybeacons and lighted and unlighted buoys.
> Wrecks and obstructions, such as shipwrecks, submerged rocks, and other hazards to nautical navigation.

These functions of this product work with nearly all Garmin GPS units.

Lowrance

MapCreate is Lowrance's comprehensive software for custom electronic maps and charts. More than many GPS manufacturers, Lowrance addresses the needs of boaters and mariners. It comes on a single DVD providing detail for the 48 contiguous states and Hawaii that covers:

> Rivers, lakes, and tributaries.
> More than 60,000 critical navigation aids and 10,000 wrecks and obstructions in coastal and Great Lakes waters.
> Interstate, federal, and state highways, along with interstate exit services (restaurants, lodging, fuel, auto/truck

services). Rural roads, cities and towns, railways, and key landmarks.

➤ A searchable points-of-interest database (that includes airports, hotels, restaurants, entertainment, emergency services, and more).

➤ Searchable street intersections and street addresses.

➤ National parks and forests as well as wildlife preserves, with their boundaries.

➤ Public hunting areas for 46 states.

MapCreate Series 7 is compatible with Lowrance mapping GPS+WAAS products with digital media memory card (MMC/SD) capability to accommodate loading custom maps. (Multi-Media Cards are also available with ready-to-use maps.) Besides creating the specific map areas you want, you can also control the level of detail in your maps by turning on or off map display features such as railroads or rural roads. By keeping the features you need and deactivating the ones you don't, you can maximize the usability of your custom maps while making the most efficient use of MMC memory space.

Fishing Hot Spots HotMaps are available for use with many Lowrance GPS units. Get freshwater lake and detailed fishing information. Mark prime locations for return trips and never lose your place. Each HotMaps features:

➤ Depth contours.

➤ Spot soundings.

➤ Submergent and emergent vegetation.

➤ The ability to zoom down to see detail.

➤ Hot spot indicators letting you know where the fish are!

IMS

The **IMS SmartMap** database, available on 64 region-specified cartridges covering the 48 contiguous states, allows you to zoom in for additional detail on the areas you cover most.

Included are 71,000 U.S. route and highway segments, more than 140,000 cities, over 120,000 bodies of water, and most inland waterways and coastal waters.

IMS WorldMap mini cartridges provide increased background detail to 39 popular and specific regions in Canada, Europe, Indonesia, and Australia. Each cartridge contains 1 MB of digitized mapping information, including the names and locations of towns, cities, provinces, and states; major roadways, including two- and four-lane highways; inland waterways such as public and private lakes, rivers, and streams; plus coastal hydrography, including islands and capes.

Magellan

Magellan sells a variety of mapping software products for use with many of its GPS receivers, including the Meridian series, SporTrak series, MLR, and MAP 330.

The **MapSend DirectRoute North America** software contains detailed street-level maps of the United States. Regional files can be downloaded from a PC to compatible Magellan GPS receivers. Map details include streets, lakes, rivers, coastlines, parks, hunting and fishing, railways, and points of interest for the United States. Regions and level of detail are user controllable. The software allows you to set your own waypoints and routes on your PC, edit them, and download them to the GPS receiver.

The **MapSend Topo** software contains detailed 3-D topographic maps that can be downloaded from your PC to your GPS receiver. Map details again include streets, lakes, rivers, coastlines, parks, railways, and points of interest for the United States. Topographic details include points of interest such as summits, wells, towers, and dams. Topography is derived from the U.S. government's digital elevation model (DEM). The software allows you to set your own waypoints and routes on your PC, then edit and download them to the GPS receiver.

MAP PROGRAMS THAT WORK WITH MULTIPLE TYPES OF GPS RECEIVERS

ChartTiff

ChartTiff (http://www.charttiff.com) sells a wide variety of standard and custom digital and paper maps and aerial photographs derived mostly from USGS maps and data sets. Products are geared primarily to users who want to print their own maps, acquired on either CD or the Internet. A wide range of scales, grids, and map sizes are available.

OziExplorer

OziExplorer (http://www.oziexplorer.com/) is an interactive, raster-image, trip-planning, and moving map software package. *Ozi* is short for Australian, the country of origin for this useful program. It allows you to add waypoints, routes, and tracks to a map, then download them to a GPS receiver. With this software, you can:

> Scan and calibrate your own maps or charts.
> Use maps in various formats that can be purchased in digital form (BSB, MapTech, USGS DRG).
> Enjoy direct support for most Lowrance/Eagle, Garmin, and Magellan GPS receivers for uploading and downloading way-points, routes, and tracks.
> Upload and download events for Lowrance/Eagle GPS receivers.
> Create tracks on the map and upload to the GPS (Lowrance/Eagle, Garmin, and Magellan). Not all GPS models support this function.
> Specify permanent map features and display a picture for each feature. Place symbols and comments on the map.
> Enjoy support for more than 100 map datums and numerous map projections.
> Use numerous grid systems, including UTM, BNG, IG, Swiss, Swedish, and NZG.
> Print maps and waypoint lists.

Fugawi

The Fugawi (http://www.fugawi.com) software can be used to create accurate digital maps from any scanned map or existing map database (such as BSB Marine Charts or USGS Topographic Maps). Then, in real-time navigation mode, your position is displayed on the map as you move and new maps are automatically loaded as you travel to new areas. North American customers receive detailed street maps of the entire United States on DVD that includes a 3D capability that enables the user to "fly" over the 3D map. Like most map programs, Fugawi allows you to position way-points and routes on your map with a click of the mouse and then upload them to your GPS receiver for use in the field. After returning home you can reverse the process and download added way-points, routes, and tracks onto the digital maps.

The program corrects scanned maps for rotation, skewing, and differential stretching of the axes caused by photocopying or paper shrinkage. It supports ready-made marine charts, land maps, and street maps and automatically imports BSB, MapTech, SoftChart, ChartTiff, USGS DRG, and TIF+TFW digital map products. Fugawi provides real-time GPS navigation with a GPS-equipped Palm PDA (an operating system of 3.5 or higher is required). Select an area of a map and press the *hot-sync* button.

MapTech, Inc.

MapTech, Inc.'s (http://www.maptech.com), digital mapping business encompasses navigation software; digital, nautical and aeronautical charts; and topographic maps. It also produces paper marine chart and guide products. MapTech began producing raster USGS topographic maps in 1996. MapTech also offers "content" products that add value to its raster maps and charts. Land topographic maps have elevation data and place names.

MapTech's Terrain Navigator offers topographic map coverage for the entire United States with up to 300 quads per CD, in two scales—1:24/25,000 (7.5' series) and 1:100,000. It is available by state; smaller states are grouped into regions. Special sets are available of U.S. national parks, the Pacific Coast Trail, the Continental Divide, and the Appalachian Trail.

With this software, you can:

> Find maps quickly by using the graphical index map or searching by map name, lat/long, zip code, or more than 50 types of place-names such as rivers and summits.
> Find exact coordinates (lat/long, UTM, MGRS) instantly.
> View digital USGS maps in 2-D or 3-D, or both at the same time in a split screen. Spin, tilt, and view 3-D images from any angle. There are multiple 3-D viewing options, including daylight, fog, white, moonlight, wire frame, overhead, or glasses. The wire frame view, for example, lets you visualize the interior of the terrain as well as the surface. White view transforms only the elevation data from a selected area into three dimensions.
> Use the seamless mode to stitch multiple maps into a single, continuous map. This allows you to view and print from four maps at once. Or, you can view maps with collars—that is, borders with detailed map information.
> Annotate maps with markers, routes, and tracks. You can create routes directly on the maps. You can adjust waypoint locations, add or remove waypoints, and select individual symbols and colors to represent each waypoint, segment, or leg of a route.
> Create elevation and line-of-sight graphs that include elevation gain and loss calculations. The elevation profile tool allows you to view cross-section terrain profiles.
> Measure distance and area quickly, even across multiple maps.
> Enjoy complete documentation, online tutorials, and a USGS map symbol reference guide.

- Transfer marks, routes, and tracks from your PC into popular GPS receivers.
- Transfer marks, routes, and tracks from your GPS back to your Terrain Navigator to analyze where you've been on a detailed map.
- Connect a GPS to a laptop and turn it into a moving map display.
- The MapTech software is compatible with Pocket Navigator for Pocket PC handhelds (sold separately). Connect a GPS receiver, and you'll see your position right on the screen. Outdoor Navigator provides the same functionality for PDAs running on Palm OS 4 and OS 5.
- Create customized printouts with optional lat/long grids, UTM grids, and compass alignment guide.
- Print maps on standard office printers, with or without the USGS borders and legend.
- Enjoy print quality comparable to original USGS paper topos.

Pharos

Pharos (http://www.pharosgps.com) markets GPS receivers specifically designed to integrate with PDAs. It also sells OSTIA, a full-feature GPS-ready navigation software package for Pocket PC devices that includes complete street-level U.S. and Canadian map coverage. It offers real-time tracking and point-to-point routing, voice-prompted driving directions, turn-by-turn directions, one-touch reroute, searching by address, intersection, or points of interest, and fast zoom.

TeleType GPS

TeleType (http://www.teletype.com) software includes street-level maps for the entire United States, Canada, or Europe. In addition to streets, TeleType GPS also displays rivers, lakes, oceans, and parks. An average-sized U.S. state uses about 15 MB of space on your computer. You can choose to load entire states or just portions of states to your handheld device. Door-to-door routing, with visual and voice instructions, can be accomplished over large geographic areas, even coast to coast.

TeleType GPS lets you:

- Zoom in and out for all maps.
- Display current position coordinates.
- Perform door-to-door routing on PDAs and laptops with rerouting if you get off track.
- Choose between human and synthesized voice for voice alerts of upcoming turns, and customize alerts to city or highway travel.
- Display lakes and rivers.
- Plot routes that span multiple states.
- Route using preferences such as via highways.
- Create your own unlimited number of waypoints, search by waypoint name, and attach photos to waypoints.
- Store frequently used addresses and routes.
- Selectively show or hide waypoints by route (folder).
- Easily export maps from desktop computer to handheld computer via either main memory or storage card.
- Import your own scanned maps.

Other features include:

- GPS moving map software and maps.
- Supports for Windows CE, Windows 98/ME/2000/XP, Pocket PC.
- Support for turn restrictions—it knows about one-way streets!
- Complete waypoint entry and management.
- Terraserver map support.
- World file support.
- More than three million points of interest, including restaurants, hotels, ATMs, gas stations, hospitals, public

and governmental buildings, and more, all searchable by name.

> UTM grid support.
> Distance measuring and course direction.
> Automatic map loading.
> Trip route recording and replaying.
> Trip route export.
> Metric/English scale units.

U.S. Geological Survey

Part of the Department of the Interior, the USGS (http://www.usgs. gov/) publishes a vast range of continually evolving paper and digital maps. Many of its public data sets have been repackaged by commercial vendors to meet the needs of various markets, including the outdoor market. The USGS mapping Web site at (http://mapping.usgs.gov/) provides access to extensive descriptions of the many mapping product available from the USGS, including where they can be purchased online or over the counter. The EarthExplorer Web site (http://edcsns17.cr.usgs.gov/Earth Explorer/) provides information about available satellite images, aerial photographs, and cartographic products available from the USGS and instructions on how to order them. The MAPFINDER Web site (http://edc.usgs.gov/Webglis/glisbin/finder_main.pl?dataset_name=MAPS_LARGE) provides a quick and easy way to order 7.5' topographic maps. The PHOTOFINDER Web site provides a quick and easy way to find and order USGS National Aerial Photography Program (NAPP) photos. These photographs, taken on roughly a five-year cycle and produced to rigorous specifications, cover the entire lower 48 states. The photos are shot from airplanes flying at 20,000 feet. Each 9-by9-inch photo (without enlargement) covers an area a bit more than 5 miles on a side.

Many USGS products are available from regional mapping centers, listed below.

Earth Resources Observation Systems
(EROS) Data Center
47914 252nd Street
Sioux Falls, SD 57198-0001
605-594-6511
http://edc.usgs.gov/

Mapping Applications Center (MAC)
567 National Center
12201 Sunrise Valley Drive
Reston VA 20192
703-648-5953
http://mac.usgs.gov/

Mid-Continent Mapping Center (MCMC)
1400 Independence Road, MS 231
Rolla, MO 65401-2602
573-308-3500
http://mcmcweb.er.usgs.gov/

Rocky Mountain Mapping Center (RMMC)
DFC Mailstop 510
P.O. Box 25046
Denver, CO 80225-0046
303-202-4000
http://rmmcweb.cr.usgs.gov/

Western Mapping Center (WMC)
345 Middlefield Road, MS 532
Menlo Park, CA 94025
650-329-4390
http://www-wmc.wr.usgs.gov/

MAP SOFTWARE FOR PDAS AND NOTEBOOKS

Delorme

DeLorme (http://www.delorme.com), a long-established mapping business, has a wide range of regularly updated products.

STREET ATLAS USA 2008

Street Atlas USA 2008 is the update of Delorme's established Street Atlas USA program. It incorporates a variety of new techniques and data sources, including the most recent U.S. Census street data and custom DeLorme data sets. Operating on a notebook PC, this software is great for the on the road portion of your trip.

The 2008 edition covers 6.2 million streets across the United States plus 4.2 million places of interest—the most extensive library of listings available, according to DeLorme. It will help you find hotels, restaurants, banks, schools, colleges, attractions, and much more. You can search for anyplace in the nation using *quicksearch* and *advanced search* options, and create automatic address-to-address routes using *shortest distance* or *quickest time* settings.

This software can be used with DeLorme and other GPS brands connected to a laptop to track yourself in real time on split-screen maps showing detailed street-level and wide-area positions at the same time. Issue spoken commands such as "Where am I?" and "How far to the next turn?" and the computer answers you. You can find the nearest conveniences from your current position and route to them. *Turn details* offers zoomed-in map views showing each turn along your route. *Route directions* shows left and right, as well as north, south, east, and west directional indicators.

Street Atlas USA also has extensive drawing tools. Choose from the many included symbols to add custom notes to your maps. Easily move and delete your custom notes. Add lines, polygons, and other shapes. Checkboxes allow you to turn on and off route drawing layers, custom note layers, and more.

TOPO USA 7.0

Topo USA 7.0 provides complete U.S. coverage on one DVD-ROM. Besides looking at the maps on screen, you can print them to a size as large as 3 feet by 3 feet on an ordinary printer (you then assemble the pieces). Track your position in real time using a DeLorme Earthmate GPS Receiver connected to a laptop, on both 2-D and 3-D maps. You can also track in 3-D using separately available satellite imagery. It's compatible with Garmin, Magellan, and other GPS receivers.

Features include:

> Automatic trail or street routing.
> The ability to add your own mutable roads and trails.
> Split-screen 2-D and 3-D side-by-side map viewing, including recent satellite imagery and other DeLorme map data sets.
> Elevation profiles of routes, roads, trails, and other features.
> Updated vector-based topographic maps that provide more recent information and versatility than products that simply scan raster maps.
> More than 300,000 miles of updated trails, including national parks and ranger districts.

7.5-MINUTE QUAD MAPS

For years, people who spend a lot of time outdoors have been accustomed to the ubiquitous 1:24,000 scale USGS 7.5' "quad" maps. They are now available in electronic form from many sources, but the DeLorme state-by-state sets (a few big states are broken into multiple sets, and some smaller ones are combined) provide added viewing features. A total of 1,525 maps (7.5' each) is required to cover all of Kansas (some maps overlap into adjacent states). At $6 each for the printed hard copy, that's a total of $9,150. You could download individual files in digital raster graphic (DRG) format from one of several public sources, but you would need to provide your own viewing software. This $100 DVD for the whole state therefore looks like a steal.

In addition to the raster quad maps that can be viewed at 17 zoom levels, the DVD includes 80 viewing levels of De-

Lorme's extensive 1999 road and topographic vector. You can scroll seamlessly through quad after quad. No more cutting and pasting incongruous paper quad maps together. Print exactly the area maps you want. You can also find what you need by searching for quads, geographic features, placenames, street addresses, latitude/longitude coordinates, and more.

Gain an instant perspective of the terrain to assess groundwater flow, trail difficulty, or land-use opportunities. Preview your destination in detailed 3-D. Adjust the pitch and rotate the 3-D views to examine the terrain in a whole new dimension. Profile elevation changes; show terrain distance and horizontal distance. Measure distances in feet or meters, and calculate areas in square feet, acres, or hectares.

You can also display features such as new roads, trails, flood-plains, and areas of commercial or residential growth with the drawing tools—then include such details on the map by adding MapNotes, symbols, lines, polygons, arcs, rectangles, splines, and circles.

QUAD Maps works on laptops. Connect to most popular GPS receivers—including DeLorme's Earthmate—and track your position in real time. Export maps to popular handheld computers (XMap Handheld software is required, for an extra charge).

Save the latitude/longitude waypoints for a location with your stand-alone GPS receiver, download them to the software, and see their locations on QUAD Maps.

SAT 10

DeLorme's SAT 10 is 10-meter-resolution natural-color satellite imagery derived from merging SPOT 10-meter panchromatic and Landsat 30-meter multispectral scenes. The data has been tonal balanced and edge matched to create a mosaic image across each state. The scenes were geo-registered using ground control points from the USGS 7.5' topo maps and ortho-corrected using USGS digital elevation model.

Most of the scenes used were taken in 2000 and 2001, with no scenes older than 1998.

Topo USA 7.0 (described above) or XMap (which we'll get to in a moment) is required to view SAT 10 imagery. With either program you can view the satellite data on one side of your computer screen, and the 3-D TopoQuads data (sold separately) on the other. The linked map views make it easy to update the USGS 7.5' topo maps. While these maps are an industry standard, the average map is more than 20 years old. With SAT 10 imagery, new roads stand out brightly against the vegetation; use the drawing tools to trace these new features, and you have updated and annotated quad maps.

XMAP

XMap (the current version is 5.2) allows you to view SAT 10 satellite photos and 3-D TopoQuads side by side. One of the frustrating features of DeLorme's great map software is that it has often been difficult to print on paper what you see on screen. XMap supports all types of printers, from the inexpensive desktop to large-format plotters. Mural-map tools allow you to create large posters from multiple 8.5-by-11-inch sheets, or piece together large plots to make custom maps tailored to your trip. The ability to include the coordinate system of your choice is particularly useful. You can do real-time tracking with most GPS receivers and upload and download tracks to many—a feature we have found useful when we want to plan a trip with more detailed information than most GPS vendor software provides.

OTHER INTERESTING MAP SOURCES

Google Maps

Google Maps have become familiar to most internet surfers, and with good reason: they are outstanding, no-cost street maps of many, but not all, of the world's countries. For the

US they are comprehensive and dependable. Don't miss the options to switch to Satellite and Terrain views, or the amazing "Street View" of selected cities, which displays a 360-degree photograph of the point on the map you designate. Google Maps also features a reliable Directions option for getting from point A to point B.

Mapquest

If you need a printable digital road map of a small area and have Web access, check out MapQuest at http://www.mapquest.com/maps/.

Omni Resources

A great map source, Omni Resources (http://www.omnimap.com/) is a major distributor of maps, globes, and teaching materials. Its specialty is international mapping, and it offers maps for nearly all countries and regions of the world, many in both paper and digital formats. With an inventory of 250,000-plus maps, Omni has one of the largest selections of international maps available in the United States.

Topo! Interactive Maps

This digital map set from National Geographic is available by state, region, or for the entire United States. Seamless topographic map software covers an entire state or group of states. GPS ready and compatible with many GPS receivers, this software allows you to create routes and upload waypoints to your GPS; 3-D digital shaded relief can be toggled on and off. A right click on the level-five map will show you quad name, date, and contour interval. An optional state series upgrade is available.

You can also add enhanced map authoring tools and compatibility to handheld units (Palm and Pocket PC) with the additional purchase of TOPO! Sync USA. This allows you to add your own photos, notes, and Web links to the maps, as well as exporting maps, photos, and notes to your

Palm or Pocket PC. And it provides overview maps of the United States.

TopoZone

TopoZone (http://www.topozone.com) markets digital USGS 1:100,000, 1:63,360, 1:25,000, and 1:24,000 scale topographic map for the entire United States by annual subscription. Its service is targeted at both recreational and professional topographic map users.

This has been only a general overview of the rapidly expanding field of digital maps that can be used directly or indirectly with GPS receivers to make your time outdoors more fun. Use them where they help you, but get preoccupied with them only if you need to, or are a map junkie.

CHAPTER 9

Paper Maps and Map Sources

By now it has probably become obvious that paper maps—so called hard copy—play a very important role in successfully using GPS in outdoor recreation. In this chapter, we'll look at maps that are particularly useful for outdoor activities, explain a bit about how to use the wealth of information they provide, and tell you where to obtain them.

MAPS FOR THE OUTDOORSPERSON

Digital maps are great. They can be displayed on screen with a dynamic position indicator, often shifted to 3-D view with some hardware, and let you scroll across huge areas. And there's none of the hassle of folding or drying rain-soaked paper. Marvelous stuff but without power they are totally useless. Always take good printed maps on any outing in unfamiliar country. Even if you have a GPS unit that displays onscreen maps, take good paper maps (and a compass). Be particular about which maps you select. Make sure they have clearly marked latitude and longitude or, better yet, UTM coordinates, and preferably grids that extend across the entire map. Study them carefully to understand what information they provide. Paper maps are essential because:

> They provide a lot of information.
> They allow you to "see" a much larger area, making planning much easier.

> On long outings, you won't want to carry enough batteries to keep a GPS in operation all the time you are moving. Also, glancing at a map is usually quicker than turning on the GPS.
> A GPS receiver is a complex electronic device. Anything electronic can fail, get broken, or get lost. Murphy's Law ensures that eventually all these will happen.

Datums, grids, and coordinate systems were discussed in chapter 3. Let's review several other important characteristics of maps.

PROJECTION

Projection is the system of parallels and meridians used to draw the earth's three-dimensional surface on a flat piece of paper. Each type of projection results in some distortion. The two-dimensional map differs in some degree from the real surface it is attempting to describe in four ways: distance, direction, shape, and area. Distortion is absent on the map only along the line where the flat surface onto which the planetary sphere is projected intersects the sphere. Different projections minimize a particular type of distortion, making them more suitable for certain uses and less so for others.

> **Equal-area projection:** The shapes of the continents and directions (north, south, east, west) are distorted, but the sizes of the continents in relation to one another are correct.
> **Conformal projection:** The shapes of the continents and directions (north, south, east, west) are correct, but the sizes are distorted. Navigators and surveyors use conformal maps because they need true shape and direction.
> **Azimuthal equidistant projection:** The distance between two points on a straight line can be measured accurately. Airplanes use equidistant projections.
> **Compromise projection:** The shapes of the continents and directions (north, south, east, west) are distorted, but in a balanced way. Many maps use compromise projections.

USGS MAP SCALES

MAP SERIES	SCALE	I INCH EQUALS	I CENTIMETER EQUALS (approx)	SIZE (latitude x longitude)	AREA (square miles)
Puerto Rico 7.5'	1:20,000	1,667 feet	200 meters	7.5' × 7.5'	71
7.5'	1:24,000	2,000 feet (exact)	240 meters	7.5' × 7.5'	49–70
7.5'	1:25,000	2,083 feet	250 meters	7.5' × 7.5'	49–70
7.5' × 15'	1:25,000	2,083 feet	250 meters	7.5' × 15'	98–140
USGS/ DMA 15'	1:50,000	4,166 feet	500 meters	15' × 15'	197–282
15'	1:62,500	1 mile	625 meters	15' × 15'	197–282
Alaska 1:63,500	1:63,500	1 mile (exact)	633.6 meters	15' × 20'–36'	207–281
County 1:50,000	1:50,000	4,166 feet	500 meters	County	Varies
County 1:100,000	1:100,000	1.6 miles	1 kilometer	County	Varies
30' × 60'	1:100,000	1.6 miles	1 kilometer	30' × 60'	1,568–2,240
U.S. 1:250,000	1:250,000	4 miles	2.5 kilometers	1' × 2'–3'	4,580–8,669
State maps	1:500,000	8 miles	5 kilometers	State	Varies
U.S. 1:1,000,000	1:1,000,000	16 miles	10 kilometers	4' × 6'	73,734–102,759
U.S. sectional	1:2,000,000	32 miles	20 kilometers	State groups	Varies

SCALE: LARGE IS SMALL

Scale is the ratio of the distance over the surface of the earth to distance on the map. The level of detail shown on a map is proportionate to its scale. "The larger the number, the smaller the scale" may sound confusing, but it describes the relationship between ratio and map size. Small-scale maps—generally those with more than 4 miles per inch (1:250,000)—show less detail but greater area, appropriate for on-road use. Large-scale maps have a smaller ratio and show more detail. Large-scale maps—generally those with 1 mile or less per inch (1:63,500)—show far more detail but cover less area. You can drive all the way across one in a few minutes, but they are well suited for trail use. In between are the widely used 1:100,000 to 1:250,000 scale maps.

TYPES OF MAPS

Planimetric

Planimetric maps show only the horizontal position of information presented with no indication of terrain. They are sometimes called line maps. State highway maps are good examples of planimetric maps. They're very useful finding your way down the road but are of very limited value on the trail, particularly in complex terrain.

Topographic

The key feature that characterizes topographic maps is the use of contour lines—lines that connects points of equal elevation, usually measured in feet or meters above sea level. On large-scale maps the lines may occur in increments as small as 10 feet, while on small-scale maps they may be as much as 200 feet apart. With a bit of practice the contours come alive, revealing the slope and shape of the land they portray. Digital computer versions can actually create three-dimensional views and even allow you to visually "fly" through the landscape. Topographic maps also typically show natural and human-made features: works of nature including mountains, valleys, plains, lakes, rivers, and vegetation, as well as artificial objects such as roads, boundaries, transmission lines, and major buildings.

MAP SYMBOLS AND LEGENDS

Each mapmaker uses a series of graphical symbols and notations to provide information in a consistent, readable, and dense manner. By far the most common are those established by the U.S. Geological Survey for its topographic maps. Detailed information on how to interpret these symbols can be found in the brochure titled *Topographic Map Symbols* available from many map vendors. The USGS Web site also has a very helpful page at http://mac.usgs.gov/mac/isb/pubs/booklets/symbols/elevation.html.

An enormous variety of maps are available for the United States and in fact much of the world. The more common types useful for outdoor activities are described below.

MAPS FOR WELL-MARKED ROADS AND HIGHWAYS

Common Highway Maps and Atlases

Cruising down the federal or major state highways—most plastered with an incredibly extensive signage system—headed from one town to the next, traditional road atlases work just fine. You may not even want to bother with the GPS unless you are in areas where the signs get a bit sparse, you are using it to measure speed or distance, or you're just having fun. Maps in atlases are typically scaled at 1:500,000 up to 1:2,000,000 (8 to 35 miles per inch). Massachusetts and Montana just come out different when you display them on the same-sized page. Most atlases have an alphanumeric grid that serves as a key for locating places identified in the index. A few have latitude and longitude marks, typically microscopic in size; none we've seen has a grid. If your GPS is equipped with maps and you simply want to use the atlas to get a "bigger picture," the two may complement each other. If you are working with a more basic GPS unit, the small variable scale of the atlas makes the two difficult to use together.

One step up from the multistate atlas is the venerable single-sheet road map, available at just about every gas station and convenience store. These are a "step up" mainly because they are bigger and therefore larger in scale. Most still have alphanumeric grids, but a few have legible latitude and longitude marks. Hopefully a map publisher will soon offer state maps at a standard scale with a complete UTM grid.

USGS State Series Maps

Maps in the state series show an entire state, typically at a scale of 1:500,000, although several of the larger states are at a scale of 1:1,000,000. There are three editions of these maps: base maps, highway and contour maps (topographic edition), and shaded-relief maps. Most maps in the series show one state per sheet, but some show more than one state— New Hampshire and Vermont; Connecticut, Massachusetts, and Rhode Island; Delaware and Maryland. Four states have more than one 1:500,000 scale sheet: California (two), Michigan (two), Montana (two), and Texas (four). Alaska is the only state for which there is no 1:500,000 scale map. Alaska state maps are available at several scales, including 1:1,584,000, 1:2,500,000, 1:5,000,000, and 1:12,000,000.

These are big maps—the largest 48 by 72 inches. Printed on heavy paper, they must be carefully folded for use in a vehicle. Despite this inconvenience, they provide essential detail for use with GPS, including a lat/long grid that extends across the entire map, information on datum and projection, and contours, typically 200 feet. Section lines of the Public Land Survey System are shown, although you have to look for them. A significant weakness is that they are not updated frequently. The cost is typically $7 per map, plus shipping and handling.

Raven Maps

If you are interested in truly elegant state maps—the sort you frame for the den wall—check out Raven Maps at www.raven maps.com.

MAPS FOR BACK ROADS

Once you've left the numbered paved federal and state highways, common road maps and atlases are often of little value. Larger-scale maps with greater detail, preferably including contours, become very helpful.

State Atlases and Gazetteers

DeLorme publishes a very large-scale atlas and gazetteer for all 50 states. These atlases are carefully designed to clearly show key details of USGS topographic maps and a great deal more. Back roads, dirt roads, and many trails are clearly marked, along with lakes and streams, boat ramps, public

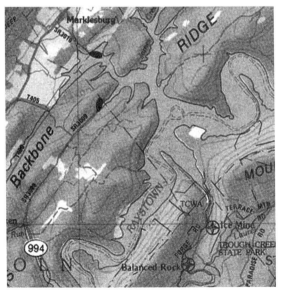

A small portion of a DeLorme atlas.

lands for recreation, land use, and land cover—forests, wetlands, agriculture, trailheads, campgrounds, and prime hunting and fishing spots. They are available individually, typically for around $20; in regional sets of five states for $75; or the entire country for $650. All atlases in the series are 11 by 15.5 inches, and the scales vary from 1:65,000 for Connecticut to 1:400,000 for Texas. Many are in the 1:150,000 to 1:250,000 range, some with a combination of scales—here, smaller-scale areas have flatter terrain and fewer features. Older editions had lat/long markings only at the corners, meaning you had to spend a lot of time creating your own grid to make them useful with a GPS. Newer editions have lat/long grids in 7' increments. Unfortunately the numbers are so incredibly small and the lines so fine anyone without perfect vision will need a magnifying glass to read them; hopefully, a UTM grid edition is forthcoming. In addition to their careful composition, a big advantage of these atlases is that they provide maps for an entire state for a very good price.

Benchmark Maps also publishes state map atlases, but they are currently available only for Arizona, California, New Mexico, Washington, Oregon, and Utah. Carefully rendered with a lot of detail, these atlases vary in scale from 1:200,000 to 1:525,000—making them useful for the highway but perhaps a bit questionable for back roads at the larger scale. Lat/long grids on the one we have used for New Mexico are at 15' increments.

USGS 1:100,000 SCALE MAPS

These maps (1.6 miles per inch) are derived from 1:24,000 scale maps, but distances and contour intervals are shown in meters. These maps cover a 30' by 60' quadrangle and are available for most of the United States and Hawaii. Highways, roads, and other human-made structures are shown, along with water features, woodland areas, and geographic names. Contours are also shown, depending on terrain relief, at intervals of 5, 10, 20, or 50 meters. They are in UTM projection, 1927 North American Datum. Lat/long grid ticks at 15' intervals are shown on the borders. Public Land Survey System range and section lines and numbers are clearly marked, with a 1-square-mile grid shown with a lighter line. The UTM grid is marked on the perimeter at 10,000-meter intervals. This grid extends across the map, although the thin black line is hard to see.

This is a wonderful series of maps. They provide an excellent navigation aid for back roads, integrate well with GPS, and have sufficient detail for use on the trail, although more is sometimes—well, often—helpful.

USGS 1:250,000 MAPS

Maps in the 1:250,000 scale series are available for the entire United States, including national parks and monuments. Originally developed by the U.S. Army Map Service during the 1950s, they are now maintained by the USGS. This series is used for many purposes, including as base maps for aeronautical charts and geologic maps and for geographic reference.

Conterminous U.S. quadrangles are 1° of latitude by 2° of longitude. Along the coasts, dimensions are modified to fit some maps. The series consists of a total of 489 sheets. The ground area shown varies with latitude, from 8,218 square miles at 30° N to 6,222 square miles at 49° N. Sheet size is generally about 32 by 22 inches.

The Alaska reconnaissance series containing 153 sheets covers the mainland and adjacent islands. It is being superseded by the Alaska 1:250,000 scale series, whose maps match those in the reconnaissance series, but the source data are more accurate. Hypsographic (terrain relief) information is more generalized than on larger-scale maps. Because the contour interval is 50, 100, 200, or 500 feet, many small relief features are not shown on this series.

MAPS FOR THE TRAIL

Commercial

Many map publishers offer a range of paper maps specifically targeted at the off-road, on-trail user.

National Geographic

Those wonderful mappers at the legendary *National Geographic* magazine have long published a steady stream of great maps (http://maps.nationalgeographic.com/trails/). We own boxes of them and regularly buy more at garage and library sales. Their Trails Illustrated series are specifically designed for the outdoorsperson and have become increasingly GPS friendly. Although you will have to extend the grid across the map yourself, the perimeter is marked in both lat/long and UTM grids. Printed on tear-resistant, waterproof paper, each map is an exact reproduction of USGS topographic map information—updated, customized, and enhanced to meet the unique features of each area. They fold up to about the size of a typical highway map; as a result, the scale varies, making grid readers often useless. Hiking trails, cross-country ski trails, bike trails, fishing holes, boat ramps, campgrounds, and many other items of interest are highlighted. This series focuses on national parks, forests, national monuments, BLM lands, and areas particularly attractive for mountain biking and paddle sports.

National Geographic's Adventure Series of maps cover some of the world's most exotic areas. The Nepal series includes maps of Everest Base Camp, Khumbu, Annapurna, and Lang-tang. We've yet to go, so we can't comment on their usefulness.

W. A. Fisher Company

Aficionados of the Boundary Waters, including Boundary Waters Canoe Area Wilderness (Minnesota) and Quetico Provincial Park (Ontario), have long made use of the W. A.

Fisher Company's unique maps (http://www.fishermapsmn. com/home.php). The scale varies, but perimeter grids are marked in lat/long at 5' increments so you can easily enhance and extend the maps for GPS use. Millions of modern-day voyageurs have found these maps exceedingly useful.

U.S. GOVERNMENT MAPS FOR THE TRAIL

U.S. Geological Survey Quads

The U.S. Geological Survey produces an enormous variety of maps, many useful for land navigation with a GPS. For on-the-trail use, there is no more widely available or widely used series of maps than the USGS 7.5' quadrangle series. The most common scales for these maps is 1:24,000, although 1:25,000 is used for metric editions (1 centimeter = 0.25 kilometer). Sheet size varies from 22 by 27 inches north of 31° latitude (the border between Alabama and Florida) to 23 by 27 inches south of that line. The land area covered ranges from 64 square miles at 30° N latitude (roughly Houston, Texas) and 49 square miles at 49° N latitude (the Montana border with Canada). The scale of maps for U.S. island territories varies from 1:10,000 to 1:50,000. The entire series takes around 57,000 maps.

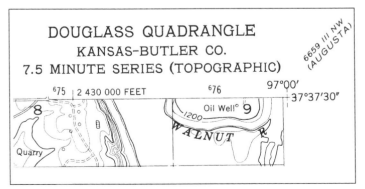

The map name and other important information is located in the upper right-hand corner of each 7.5' quad sheet.

If you are headed for the wilds of Alaska, you'll find the USGS maps a bit different. Lying much farther north, Alaska has a unique set of 15' quadrangle maps at a scale of 1:63,360 (1 inch = 1 mile). These maps typically cover 15' of latitude and from 20' to 36' of longitude. Each map shows an area of 207 to 280 square miles, depending on how far north it lies. Features shown on 15' maps are similar to those shown on 7.5' maps, except that some may be generalized or omitted because of the smaller scale. Sheet size is about 18 by 22 inches north of 62° latitude and 17 by 27 inches south of that line. The 2,920 sheets covering Alaska at this scale are completed except for about 3 percent covering the Aleutian Islands and the Bering Sea islands.

Because these maps series cover most of the United States, are widely available, and are at a scale that makes them particularly useful for the outdoorsman, a detailed discussion of the information they provide and how to take full advantage of them for land navigation with GPS technology is essential.

Map Name and Name of Adjacent Maps

Each quad map has a name based on a place or feature located within its area. The name of the quadrangle is shown at the upper right corner and again in the lower right corner, with the date of publication shown below the latter. The names of the four adjacent maps are shown along the borders in parentheses, and the names of the four maps that touch at the corners are shown printed at an angle at each corner, also in parentheses.

DOUGLASS, KANS.
N3730—W9700/7.5

1955

Quad name shown in lower right-hand corner with original date of publication. N3730 and W9700 are the latitude and longitude of the southwest (lower left) corner of the map.

Map Projection, Datum, and Date

The map projection, datum, original date of development, and date of any update—typically the same as publication—are indicated in the lower left border. Information is also provided about the grids that appear on the map.

Map Scale

The map scale, typically 1:24,000, is shown at the bottom center, as is the graphic map scale in miles, feet, and kilometers, along with the contour interval and vertical datum, typically sea level.

Map Grid

USGS 7.5' quads show three map grids as well as the Public Land Survey System.

UTM grid markings can be confusing. The vertical (northing) and horizontal (easting) UTM grid values appear at the points closest to the upper left and lower right corners, where their value are in even 1,000-meter (1-kilometer) increments. The actual grid is marked by a very thin blue tick line that extends just across the map border. The tick appears again around the border in unlabeled 1,000-meter increments. If you connect the grid ticks with solid lines as we recommend, remember that the UTM grid is not parallel to the latitude/longitude grid or, in states where the PLSS system is used, the rectilinear pattern of many roads. Adding to the confusion is the occasional absence of the blue UTM grid tick where it would conflict with other information.

The State Plane Coordinate System, while not of much use to GPS users, needs to be distinguished from the UTM markings. SPCS values are marked in the corners opposite the UTM value (lower left and upper right) with black tick marks along the border in 10,000-foot increments that are the same size as the blue UTM ticks.

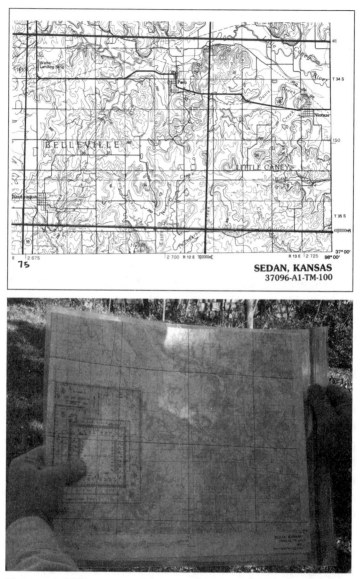

These are in UTM projection, 1927 North American Datum. Lat/Long grid ticks are at 15'.

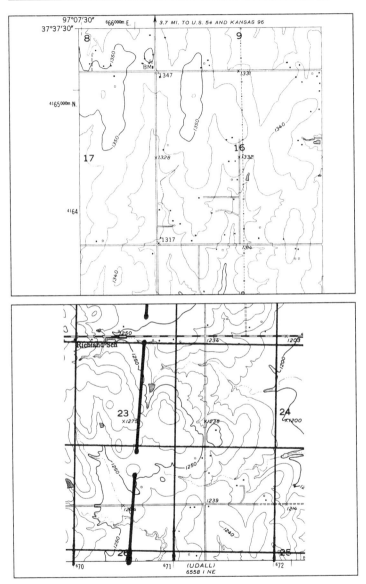

For use afield, extend the lat/long, or better yet the UTM, grid across the map by connecting tick markings of the same value. A blue indelible-ink marker works well. The heavy dashed marker line, in red on the actual map, is magnetic declination for orienting the map with magnetic north.

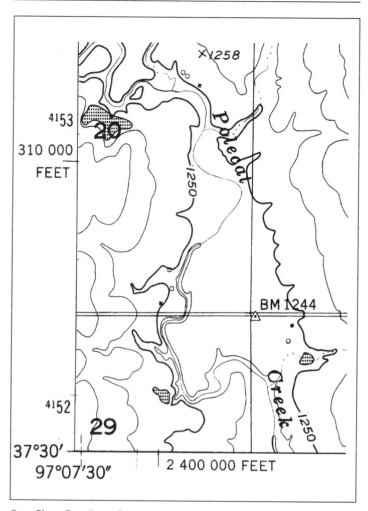

State Plane Coordinate System values are typically shown in the lower left (here 310,000 feet and 2,400,000 feet for the Kansas south zone) and the upper right with black ticks extending outside the border at 10,000-foot increments. They are of limited value to the GPS user but we point them out so you won't confuse them with other grids.

The PLSS was initiated soon after the passing of the Kansas-Nebraska Act in 1854, when a survey was commissioned by the U.S. government so that the lands newly opened for settlement could be properly and legally plotted out for the homesteaders. The survey was carried out by Charles Manners, who started by erecting a cast-iron monument on the west bluff of the Missouri River in 1855 at 40° North latitude—the northern boundary of Kansas. From this point, he surveyed 108 miles west and placed a red sandstone marker at the location of the Sixth Principal Meridian. The imaginary line between these two markers delineated the border between the two future states.

The range numbers appear in red along the top and bottom borders; township numbers appear along the vertical borders. They define 6-by-6 mile townships. The section number for each of the 36 sections, each typically (but not always) 1 square mile, is printed in red, in the center of the section if possible. Section 1 is at the upper right of the township, with numbers progressing left across the top row of the township to section 6, where numbering steps down to the next row and progressing right. The numbering continues in the fashion until section 36 is reached in the lower right corner of the township.

Magnetic Declination

Approximate mean magnetic declination is shown numerically with a graphic indicating direction on the lower border. Use the numeric value, not the graph, to project a line of declination across the map, and recall that if the map is several decades old the declination may have changed significantly. Information on adjusting for magnetic declination is provided in chapter 11. This diagram will also show how much the UTM grid, marked GN, differs from true north. If the location is to the left of the central meridian of the UTM zone, grid north (GN) will be to the left (west) of true north. Conversely, if the location is to the right of the central meridian of the zone, GN will be to the right (east) of true north.

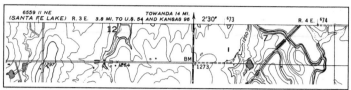

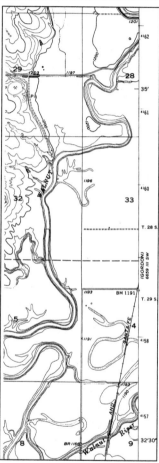

R. 3 E. and R. 4 E. (in red on the actual map) along the top border indicate the six-mile-wide column, equal to the width of a 36-square-mile township, which the Public Land Survey System refers to as Ranges. The E stands for "east," or the fourth range east of the Sixth Principal Meridian, about 94.4° West longitude (an odd number with an interesting history). The PLSS does not line up with the UTM grid or the lat/long grid, so map borders cut through one square-mile section. The 12 and 7 section numbers that would normally appear in the center of the section have been moved down, allowing them to appear on the clipped section. Section 12 is the rightmost section of the second row down from the top in Range 3, while section 7 is the leftmost section in the second row down in Range 4. The 673 and 674 labeled ticks, (blue on the actual map) mark the UTM vertical grid line or Eastings. Since the central longitude line for the UTM zone (14 for this map) has a false Easting of 500,000, the 673 means the line is 173,000 meters to the East of the zone's central meridian. Note that the ticks for 671 and 672 are printed but not labeled to avoid clutter. The 2' 30" longitude value is added to the 97° 00' value that appears in the upper right-hand corner.

The T.28 S. and T 29 S. (also in red on the actual map) along the side border indicate the six mile horizontal band of sections the PLSS refers to as townships. S is for "south," the 28th township south of the 40° N parallel of longitude or baseline. Again, you can determine the line between the two by the nonsequential section numbers. UTM grid ticks are shown, with the 4157 indicating 4,157,000 meters north of the equator. The 32' 30" latitude is added to the 37° shown in the lower right and left corners.

Other USGS Maps

USGS County Maps

The USGS publishes a series of county maps at a scale of 1:50,000 or 1:100,000, although only about 20 percent of the counties in the country are currently available. About half of those are at a scale of 1:50,000, making them quite useful for trail use. The other half are at a scale of 1:10,000. The content of the 1:50,000 scale maps is similar to 1:24,000 quadrangle maps. There is considerably less detail on the 1:100,000 county maps.

USGS National Park Maps

The USGS has an extensive series of topographic maps of national parks, national monuments, and other units of the National Park Service, many with shaded relief. These maps highlight recreational facilities and range in scale from 1:960 for the map of the Franklin D. Roosevelt National Historic Site in New York, to 1:250,000 for the map of the Denali National Park in Alaska. Sheet size ranges from about 21 by 17 inches on up to 61 by 46 inches

U.S. Forest Service

The forest service, part of the U.S. Department of Agriculture, is a federal agency that manages public lands in national forests and grasslands. National forests and grasslands are America's great outdoors, totaling over 191 million acres, an area roughly equivalent to the state of Texas. Needless to say, it publishes maps of the land it manages.

Visitor maps are available for each national forest and grassland. These maps provide forest wide information on attractions, facilities, services, and opportunities and are available to purchase at the visitor centers of individual forests, regional offices, the U.S. Geological Survey, and many retail outlets. They are useful for trip planning.

The forest service maps—1:126,720 scale (½ inch = 1 mile)—provide information, in addition to that available on a USGS topographic map, on recreational uses, local plants and wildlife, trails, roads, streams, lakes, visitor centers, facilities available, campgrounds, and picnic areas. The maps also display color photographs of points of interest and activities. Each map covers all or part of one national forest. These maps are useful for trip planning and general forest or grassland information. The more detailed USGS maps are preferable if your trip requires careful land navigation. Forest service maps can also be purchased online for $7.50 ($9 plastic coated), plus shipping and handling, by going to http://rockyweb.cr.usgs.gov/forestservice/index.html. Specialty maps and brochures are available for many individual forests covering specific trails, wilderness areas, and other special areas.

U.S. Bureau of Land Management

The Bureau of Land Management (BLM), part of the U.S. Department of the Interior, administers 262 million acres of public lands, located primarily in 12 western states. That is a lot of land, and BLM publishes maps of it.

The agency's National Resource (Public) Land Maps, at a scale of 1:500,000, show state and federal ownership (forest service, BLM, park service, and Indian and military reservations) in color, as well as township and range designations. The overall size is 52 by 44 inches. These are not really navigation maps, but they are useful for identifying trip opportunities, general planning, and identifying which 1:100,000 scale maps may be useful.

Most useful for the outdoorsman are the intermediate-scale (1:100,000) 30' by 60' (about 30 by 50 miles) quadrangle maps showing contours and elevations in meters/feet, highways, roads, and other human-made structures, water features, geographic names, and federal surface and mineral ownership. Maps in this series are 42 by 30 inches and include township, range, and section designations. They can be ordered directly from individual state BLM offices at a cost of $4 plus shipping. To find the state office online, enter www.**.blm.gov in a Web browser, substituting the two-letter state abbreviation for the **. Offices are maintained in Alaska (AK), Arizona (AZ), California (CA), Colorado (CO), Idaho (ID), Montana (MT), Nevada (NV), New Mexico (NM), Oregon (OR) (includes Washington State), Utah (UT), and Wyoming (WY). These sites are also great sources of information about recreational opportunities and campsite reservation requirements. Online map purchases are, however, generally not available. BLM maps of many western states can be purchased online from the private Public Lands Information Center for $7 at http://66.96.174.47/content/home. shtml.

National Park Service

The national park system encompasses approximately 83.6 million acres, of which about 4.3 million acres are in private ownership. The system includes a wide range of assets, including national parks; national monuments; national preserves, historic sites, and parks; national memorials, battlefields, and cemeteries; national recreation areas; national seashores, lakeshores, and rivers; national parkways and trails. Among them are many of America's greatest outdoor recreation opportunities. There are many maps available to help you enjoy them.

National Park Service Cartographic Resources Visitor Use Maps in printable Adobe portable document (*.pdf) format are available over the Web for most National Park Service sites at http://www.nps.gov/carto/data.html. While somewhat useful for planning purposes, these maps are little more than diagrams with no scale or grid, making them of little value for use with a GPS for land navigation.

The USGS also publishes topographic maps of many national parks. A complete list is on the Web at http://mac.usgs.gov/mac/isb/pubs/forms/natl-parks.html.

WHERE TO FIND USGS MAPS

Good maps are easy to find if you don't wait until the last minute. USGS paper maps can be ordered online from a number of sources. The USGS advises that the fastest way to acquire its maps, digital or paper, is often from a commercial source, and they provide a detailed online list of vendors at http://rocky-web.cr.usgs.gov/acisbin/querypartner.cgi. Most of these vendors stock only maps for their immediate area or state. Visit http://mac.usgs.gov mac/ maplists/ online to identify which maps are available for your area of interest. Free index maps showing which maps cover a particular area and map catalogs are available by state. Contact the ESIC (see below) nearest you or order online. USGS primary series topographic maps (1:24,000, 1:25,000, 1:63,360 scales) cost $6 per sheet. Most other topographic maps cost $7 per sheet. Commercial vendors may charge more.

USGS Earth Science Information Centers (ESIC)
ESICs provide information and sales service for USGS maps.

ANCHORAGE—ESIC
U.S. Geological Survey
4230 University Drive
Room 101
Anchorage, AK 99508-4664
TELEPHONE: (907) 786-7011
FAX: (907) 786-7050
EMAIL: gfdurocher@usgs.gov
HOURS:
Monday through Friday
8:30 A.M.–4:30 P.M.
(Alaska Time)

DENVER—ESIC
U.S. Geological Survey
Box 25286
Building 810
Denver Federal Center
Denver, CO 80225
TELEPHONE: (303) 202-4200
FAX: (303) 202-4188
EMAIL: infoservices@usgs.gov
HOURS:
Monday through Friday
8:00 A.M.–4:00 P.M.
(Mountain Time)

USGS INFORMATION SERVICES
(Map and Book Sales)
Box 25286
Denver Federal Center
Denver, CO 80225
TELEPHONE: (303) 202-4700
FAX: (303) 202-4693
HOURS:
Monday through Friday
8:00 A.M.–4:00 P.M.
(Mountain Time)

USGS INFORMATION SERVICES
(Open-File Report Sales)
Box 25286
Denver Federal Center
Denver, CO 80225
TELEPHONE: (303) 202-4700
FAX: (303) 202-4188
HOURS:
Monday through Friday
8:00 A.M.–4:00 P.M.
(Mountain Time)

MENLO PARK—ESIC
U.S. Geological Survey
Building 3, MS 532
Room 3128
345 Middlefield Road
Menlo Park, CA 94025-3591
TELEPHONE: (650) 329-4309
FAX: (650) 329-5130
EMAIL: wmcesic@usgs.gov
HOURS:
Monday through Friday
8:00 A.M.–4:00 P.M.
(Pacific Time)

RESTON—ESIC
U.S. Geological Survey
507 National Center
Reston, VA 20192
TELEPHONE: (703) 648-5953
FAX: (703) 648-5548
TDD: (703) 648-4119
EMAIL: ask@usgs.gov
HOURS:
Monday through Friday
8:00 A.M.–4:00 P.M.
(Eastern Time)

ROLLA—ESIC
U.S. Geological Survey
1400 Independence Road
MS 231
Rolla, MO 65401-2602
TELEPHONE: (573) 308-3500
FAX: (573) 308-3615
EMAIL: mcmcesic@usgs.gov
HOURS:
Monday through Friday
7:45 A.M.–4:15 P.M.
(Central Time)
Tours available
Tuesday through Thursday,
9:00 A.M.–3:30 P.M.

SIOUX FALLS—ESIC
U.S. Geological Survey
EROS Data Center
Sioux Falls, SD 57198-0001
TELEPHONE: (605) 594-6151
FAX: (605) 594-6589
TDD: (605) 594-6933
EMAIL: custserv@usgs.gov
HOURS:
Monday through Friday,
8:00 A.M.–4:00 P.M.
(Central Time)

ONLINE MAPS FOR THE TRAIL

Offroute

Offroute has a large inventory of standard USGS paper maps, but more interestingly it will print a custom topographic map for you of the specific area you define on its Web site. Go to http://www.offroute.com. In the United States as you zoom down to a view of 20 square miles, detailed, topographic images appear, allowing you to pinpoint your area of interest. By selecting a particular map or book product, the boundaries of the product are displayed, allowing you to see what area each map or book product actually covers. At the lowest zoom level of 10 miles you are viewing a 1:250,000 scale topographic map—detailed enough to plan a basic route in the backcountry. Maps can be printed at standard 1:24,000 or 1:30,750 in several sizes. The 13-by-18-inch or 26-by-36-inch maps are suitable for field use, while the bigger 26-by-36- and 36-by-50-inch are suitable for planning or wall hanging. Offroute will print on waterproof paper or laminate, and provides the additional option of overprinting the lat/long or UTM grid—great for GPS use. You could do the same thing by purchasing map software, if you have a color plotter. Or you could buy much cheaper paper maps, cut out the section of interest, and tape or glue them together. We always want a good paper map, and for our next high adventure we plan to order a custom model: the right area, the best scale, and the correct grid—extended across the entire map.

Map Town

Map Town carries topographic maps of Canada at scales of both 1:50,000 and 1:250,000, as well as many other map and GPS products. It retail store is open 8:00 A.M.–6:00 P.M. Monday through Friday, 10:00 A.M.–5:00 P.M. Saturday.

100-400 Fifth Avenue SW, Calgary, Alberta, Canada T2P OL6
Email: maps@maptown.com; Ph. #: (403) 266-2241
Fax #: (403) 266-2356; Toll Free Ph #: (1-877-921-6277)
Toll Free Fax #: (1-877-776-2356)

DISTANCE AND AREA UNITS AND CONVERSION

Travel requires the use of units of distance (or length) and occasionally area. Understanding the dimension of common units and how to convert between them is helpful. Knowing something about their origin may not be all that important but it adds considerable pleasure to the process. Russ Rowlett at the University of North Carolina at Chapel Hill has a wonderful Web page titled How Many? A Dictionary of Units of Measurement at http://www.unc.edu/-rowlett/units/custom.html in which he relates the history of measurement units. Excerpts on distance and area units are quoted below.

Inch—Foot—Yard

The **inch** represents the width of a thumb; in fact, in many languages, the word for "inch" is also the word for "thumb." The **foot** (12 inches) was originally the length of a human foot, although it has evolved to be longer than most people's feet. The **yard** (3 feet) seems to have gotten its start in England as the name of a 3-foot measuring stick, but it is also understood to be the distance from the tip of the nose to the end of the middle finger of the outstretched hand.

Furlong—Mile—Nautical Mile

. . . all land in England was traditionally measured by the **gyrd** or **rod**, an old Saxon unit probably equal to 20 "natural feet." The Norman kings had no interest in changing the length of the rod, since the accuracy of deeds and other land records depended on that unit. Accordingly, the length of the rod was fixed at 5.5 yards (16.5 feet). This was not very convenient, but 5.5 yards happened to be the length of the rod as measured by the 12-inch foot, so nothing could be done about it. In the Saxon land-measuring system, 40 rods make a **furlong** (fuhrlang), the length of the traditional furrow (fuhr) as plowed by ox teams on Saxon farms. These ancient Saxon units, the rod and the furlong, have come down to us today with essentially no change. Longer distances in England are traditionally measured in miles.

The **mile** is a Roman unit, originally defined to be the length of 1,000 paces of a Roman legion. A "pace" here means two steps, right and left, or about 5 feet, so the mile is a unit of roughly 5,000 feet. For a long time no one felt any need to be precise about this, because distances longer than a furlong did not need to be measured exactly. It just didn't make much difference whether the next town was 21 or 22 miles away. In medieval England, various mile units seem to have been used. Eventually, what made the most sense to people was that a mile should equal 8 furlongs, since the furlong was an English unit roughly equivalent to the Roman **stadium** and the Romans had set their mile equal to 8 stadia. This correspondence is not exact: The furlong is 660 English feet and the stadium is only 625 slightly shorter Roman feet.

In 1592, Parliament settled this question by setting the length of the mile at 8 furlongs, which works out to 1,760 yards or 5,280 feet. This decision completed the English distance system. Since this was just before the settling of the American colonies, British and American distance units have always been the same.

The **nautical mile** is defined to be the average distance on the earth's surface represented by 1' of latitude. This may seem odd to landlubbers, but it makes good sense at sea, where there are no mile markers but latitude can be measured. Because the earth is not a perfect sphere, it is not easy to measure the length of the nautical mile in terms of the statute mile used on land. For many years the British set the nautical mile at 6,080 feet (1,853.18 meters), exactly 800 feet longer than a statute mile; this unit was called the Admiralty mile. Until 1954 the U.S. nautical mile was equal to 6,080.20 feet (1,853.24 meters). In 1929 an international conference in Monaco redefined the nautical mile to be exactly 1,852 meters or 6,076.11549 feet, a distance known as the international nautical mile. The international nautical mile equals about 1.1508 statute miles. There are usually 3 nautical miles in a league. The unit is designed to equal 1/60 degree, although actual degrees of latitude vary from about 59.7 to 60.3 nautical miles.

Acre

In all the English-speaking countries, land is traditionally measured by the acre, a very old Saxon unit that is either historic or archaic, depending on your point of view. There are references to the **acre** at least as early as the year 732. The word acre also meant "field" and as a unit an acre was originally a field of a size that a farmer could plow in a single day. In practice, this meant a field that could be plowed in a morning, since the oxen had to be rested in the afternoon. The French word for the unit is journal, which is derived from jour, meaning "day"; the corresponding unit in German is called the morgen ("morning") or tagwerk ("day's work").

Most area units were eventually defined to be the area of a square having sides equal to some simple multiple of a distance unit, like the square yard. But the acre was never visualized as a square. An acre is the area of a long and narrow Anglo-Saxon farm field, one furlong (40 rods) in length but only 4 rods wide. This works out, very awkwardly indeed, to be exactly 43,560 square feet. If we line up 10 of these 4 × 40 standard acres side by side, we get 10 acres in a square furlong, and since the mile is 8 furlongs there are exactly 10 × 8 × 8 = 640 acres in a **square mile**.

The Metric System

Designed during the French Revolution of the 1790s, the metric system brought order out of the conflicting and confusing traditional systems of weights and measures then being used in Europe. Prior to the introduction of the metric system, it was common for units of length, land area, and weight to vary, not just from one country to another but from one region to another within the same country. As the modern nations were gradually assembled from smaller kingdoms and principalities, confusion simply multiplied. Merchants, scientists, and educated people throughout Europe realized that a uniform system was needed, but it was only in the climate of a complete political upheaval that such a radical change could actually be considered. The metric system replaces all the traditional units, except the units of time and of angle measure, with units satisfying three conditions:

1. Only a single unit is defined for each quantity. These units are now defined precisely in the International System of Units.
2. Larger and smaller units are created by adding prefixes to the names of the defined units. These prefixes denote

powers of ten, so that metric units are always divided into tens, hundreds, or thousands. The original prefixes included milli- for 1/1,000, centi- for 1/100, deci- for 1/10, deka- for 10, hecto- for 100, and kilo- for 1,000.

3. The units are defined rationally and are related to each other in a rational fashion.

Meter

The metric units were defined in an elegant way unlike any traditional units of measure. The earth itself was selected as the measuring stick. The **meter** was defined to be one ten-millionth of the distance from the equator to the North Pole. The liter was to be the volume of one cubic decimeter, and the kilogram was to be the weight of a liter of pure water. It didn't turn out quite like this, because the scientific methods of the time were not quite up to the task of measuring these quantities precisely, but the actual metric units come very close to the design.

Hectare

An **are** is a unit of area equal to 100 square meters. The word is pronounced the same as air. Being the area of a square 10 meters on each side, the area is a little large for measuring areas indoors and a little small for measuring areas outdoors. As a result, the are is not used as often as its multiple, the hectare (ha). One are is approximately 1076.3910 square feet, 119.6000 square yards, or 0.02471 acre.

Hect- or **hecto-** is a metric prefix denoting 100, coined from the Greek word hekaton for "one hundred." **Hectare** (ha), the customary metric unit of land area, is equal to 100 acres. One hectare is a square hectometer, that is, the area of a square 100 meters on each side: approximately 107,639.1 square feet, 11,959.9 square yards, or 2.471054 acres.

CONVERSION

To Convert	Mulitiply By
Meters to feet	3.28084
Feet to meters	0.3048
Miles to kilometers	1.609344
Kilometers to miles	0.621371
Nautical miles to miles	1.150779
Miles to nautical miles	0.868976
Nautical miles to kilometers	1.852
Kilometers to nautical miles	0.539957
Acres to hectares	0.404687
Hectares to acres	2.471044
Square miles to square kilometers	2.589995
Square kilometers to square miles	0.386101

GIS Tools Online

The Bureau of Economic Geology at the Jackson School of Geosciences, the University of Texas at Austin (http://www.utexas.edu/research/beg/GIS/tools/scale2.htm), provides a useful online interactive utility that performs conversion of various units of length, area, degminsec, decdeg, scale, and degrees to radians, as well as time to GPS seconds.

To view maps online, check out this USGS site: http://mapping.usgs.gov/partners/viewonline.html.

CHAPTER 10

▶ Other Things to Think About

As you become more familiar with your GPS receiver, you may begin to think about some other issues related to using it. This chapter attempts to address a few of these issues.

USING YOUR GPS OVERSEAS

If you're one of those fortunate individuals whose outdoor recreational activities take them overseas, you might wonder if your GPS will still function in other regions of the world. The simple answer is yes, since the GPS satellites essentially cover the entire earth. There are, however, some things that you will want to consider.

If you travel overseas by air, the recent increases in airport security due to terrorist threats will require security personnel to examine your GPS receiver closely to make sure it is not a bomb or other dangerous device. You can avoid this by putting your GPS receiver into your checked baggage. Since most airlines restrict or prohibit the use of personal electronic devices, which includes GPS receivers, at least during some portions of a flight, you probably won't get to use your receiver much while on the plane anyway, and it will definitely be safer in your baggage.

Once you get to your overseas destination, you will more than likely have to reinitialize your GPS receiver. This should not be difficult, but you will want to remember to bring the operating instructions with you.

If you bring rechargeable batteries for your GPS receiver and a charger with you, you may find that your portable battery charger is not compatible with the household electrical systems common in many foreign countries. Some chargers have a switch that will allow them to work on the voltages common in foreign countries. It is best to check this out before leaving the United States, if you are going to be dependent on charging the batteries for your GPS receiver.

INSURANCE

Whether you are traveling abroad with your GPS receiver or have it stored at home while you are away, there is always the possibility of someone stealing your unit. Such a loss would generally be covered under your homeowner's or rental insurance policy, but it might be wise to check with your insurance company to verify this. If your GPS receiver is one of the higher-priced, sophisticated units that operate in conjunction with a personal computer or PDA, it might be wise to purchase a separate "valuable items" policy from your insurance agent or company. Such policies are generally available at small percentage of the cost of the insured item and can provide more coverage than is usually available under a general homeowner's or rental property policy.

LEGAL ISSUES

While we certainly hope that you will not be planning to use your GPS receiver in any activity that is obviously against the law, you should be aware of some laws that you might violate unintentionally. This would most likely be some fish or game law violation.

In some states, it is illegal to use radios or other electronic means to give information concerning the location of game animals or fish to other individuals. This regulation varies from state to state and may or may not involve GPS receivers. Obviously, anglers and hunters who plan to use a

GPS receiver should consult the laws of the state or states where they plan to do their hunting or fishing.

SAFETY

If you are headed off the road, file a trip plan with friends, just like a pilot or a mariner. Tell them:

- When you plan to leave and return.
- Where you are going, in reasonable detail.
- What type of vehicle you drive and the license number.
- What survival gear you are taking.

Give them the courtesy of a phone call or email as soon as you return.

CHAPTER 11

➤ Other Useful Tools for Finding Your Way

While a GPS receiver can be a remarkable aid to getting around outdoors, it is not the only device that can enhance your time afield. In this chapter we'll discuss some other useful devices for outdoor navigation. While some of these devices employ a lot of the same "high-tech" electronics used in GPS receivers, others are more basic forms of equipment that can still enhance your time in the outdoors.

ALTIMETERS

Altimeters are devices that allow you to determine your elevation above sea level. Although this information can be obtained from your GPS unit, the accuracy of the elevation value given by a GPS receiver is much less than the accuracy of the horizontal position values. If you need accurate elevation information, an altimeter can provide it much more precisely than your GPS unit.

Altimeters are basically barometers that relate the changes in air pressure to elevation above sea level. A variety of different types and models of altimeters are available from several different manufacturers. They range from simple aneroid-type altimeters to sophisticated electronic devices with digital displays.

COMPASSES

With the advent of so many modern electronic devices to aid us in land navigation, the old-fashioned compass may seem out of place. However, a reliable compass for backup should always be a part of any outdoors person's equipment. We'll discuss the use of compasses in more detail in the next chapter. For now it is just important to know that compass technology, like almost everything else, has improved considerably over time. While the old-style magnetic compasses are still available, they have become far more rugged and lightweight than previous models. In addition, electronic compasses with digital displays are also now on the market. Many digital compasses also include altimeters, thermometers, and other such weather-related instruments.

MAP MEASURERS

Map measurers are ingenious devices that allow you to measure distances on a map by tracing the instrument over the route proposed or taken, as shown on a map. Both mechanical

This simple mechanical map-measurement tool from Russia has an inch scale on one side and centimeters on the other. No batteries required. Run the wheel over your course and either convert the measured distance using the scale or return it to zero and run the wheel over the graphic scale bar on the map until you have covered the same distance.

and digital electronic models are available. Most such devices work by rolling a small measuring wheel along the map route. Some of the more sophisticated map measurers are capable of converting distances from one unit to another and displaying the result. For example, a particular map may have a metric scale in which a certain number of centimeters correspond to a certain number of kilometers. By choosing the appropriate units and conversions on a map measurer, however, the distance can be displayed in miles.

One such device is the digital map measurer manufactured by Brunton. Measuring 4.25 by 1.75 by 0.5 inches and weighing only 1.1 ounces, this digital map measurer provides easy calculation of distance on a map. Enter your scale and roll the end of the measurer along your map for an accurate distance readout in miles or kilometers. The device includes an eight-digit calculator, world time clock, map light, compass, and temperature measurement.

PEDOMETERS

Pedometers are devices that can be worn to give estimates of the distance traveled while walking or running. They operate by essentially counting the number of steps taken over the length of a trip. Although it may seem that such devices would not be very precise, when properly calibrated and worn they can give very accurate estimates. A variety of models are available, ranging from simple mechanical devices to those employing digital electronic technology. The pedometer market is primarily for measuring exercise, and units are available with a range of features, including distance conversion, time, stop-watch, dual walk or run mode, even estimated calorie consumption. They range in price from $10 to $50.

TWO-WAY RADIOS

The "walkie-talkies" of yesterday have grown up and become compact, sophisticated communications devices. Useful for communicating between two different groups in the same general area, these radios can also contact rescue personnel in the event of an emergency. These devices operate on the Family Radio Service (FRS) band-specific frequencies allocated to such radios. Some radios are also capable of operating on the General Radio Mobile Service (GRMS) band, which allows the radios to operate at a higher power and thus increase their range. However, operation on the GRMS band requires you to obtain a $75 license from the Federal Communications Commission. Many of theses units also contain a weather radio that allows you to pick weather broadcasts and keep alert to possible severe weather problems. At least one radio unit, the Garmin Rino, has a built-in GPS receiver. These radios may be more advantageous than cell phones in remote areas where cell coverage may not exist. They may still have difficulty operating in mountainous terrain, however, which can block signals.

SATELLITE PHONES

Modern communications, the 911 system, the shrinking sense of individual responsibility, the widespread abandonment of common sense, our increasingly litigious society—for whatever reason, many folks now seem to expect that no matter what happens, or how badly they screw up, they can and should be rescued, safe and sound. Heed the parable of the child who prayed to win the lottery. After long and intense effort by the child, God parted the clouds and yelled down, "Give me a break, buy a ticket!" If you are going to take significant risks, have medical concerns, or have legal responsibility for others and will be beyond the coverage of your cellular phone, rent a satellite phone and pack it down the trail. Phones that access the Globalstar, Iridium, and Inmarsat systems are available from many vendors. Just do a Web search for "satellite phone rental" and you'll have lots of choices. Expect to pay $70 to $100 or more per week and $1 to $4 per minute for incoming and outgoing calls. You can also buy your own satellite phone, subscribe for a monthly fee, and pay about $1.70 per minute. Some models are serious boat anchors while others are nearly as light as a cell phone. As with all sectors of the telecommunications business, it often pays quite a bit to shop. If you will be on the trail for more than the battery life of the phone, make sure to keep it turned off until you really need it.

CHAPTER 12

▶ Don't Forget Your Compass

In a world of sophisticated electronics that includes GPS receivers and their associated accessories, the old standard compass remains an important part of getting around in the outdoors. Unless you have a GPS with an integral compass, you will need a magnetic one to properly orient a map. Even with such a GPS, you will have to rely on a compass if the GPS fails for any reason. If you plan to spend time afield in areas you are not thoroughly familiar with, own a compass, learn how to use it, and carry it with you.

The compass-related information presented here represents only the bare essentials: the essentials of the modern compass, understanding the compass rose, orienting a map, accounting for declination, and finding and following a course. There is a wealth of useful information on the many subtleties of compass navigation available. When you are ready to dig further, find a copy of Bjorn Hjellström's updated classic, *Be Expert with Map & Compass*.

HOW A COMPASS WORKS

Some 2,000 years ago, the Chinese discovered that certain pieces of metal, when floated on a piece of wood, consistently pointed in a particular direction. Improvements in compass design, construction, and our understanding of the variable and constantly changing nature of the earth's magnetic field have made the simple magnetic compass an essential navigational tool. The variety of compasses available for the outdoorsman today is impressive. At the low end are devices that can barely be called toys and old, not very easy to use, military surplus models. At the other we have modern orienteering compasses that range from simple, inexpensive, and useful models, to feature-rich units and beyond.

These basic, inexpensive watch compasses are not liquid-filled and the needle jumps around a lot. Although fun, they are not serious navigation tools.

These big compasses all have roots in the military. Ranging in cost from high to modest, they are accurate and durable and particularly useful—if you plan to shoot artillery!

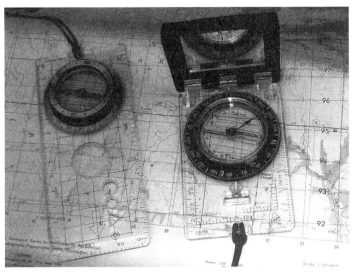

Orienteering compasses.

Today's orienteering compasses for the outdoorsman have several common features. The magnetic needle always has the north end painted red, although some also have a portion of the north needle coated with a luminous substance more easily seen in the dark. The needle sets on a point, typically a piece of sapphire, floating in a fluid that dampens movement. The compass rim atop the fluid-filled compass housing is marked with the four cardinal directions and the 360° of a circle, with 0° at north. The integral rim and housing are mounted on a clear plastic base upon which it rotates, permitting easy map orientation and course direction determination. More sophisticated models have mirrors or other aids to permit faster and more accurate use.

Perhaps the most common mistake made in using a compass is to ignore the huge error that can be caused by the presence of large metal objects. A vehicle hood or trunk is a handy spot to look at a map, but it could throw off a compass reading by as much as 90°, making it impossible to properly orient the map. Watching a couple of strong-willed outdoorsmen argue about orienting a map with their compass on the hood of their truck can be great entertainment, but gentlemen should intervene before things come to blows.

THE EARTH'S CHANGING MAGNETIC FIELD

The magnetic North Pole does not sit atop the geographic North Pole, defined by the intersection of the earth's sphere and the axis of its rotation. The earth's magnetic field is further affected by variation in the composition and movement of the earth's outer core. The angle between true north pointing to the North Pole and the direction a magnetic compass will point in a specific location is referred to as magnetic declination, or sometimes magnetic variation, compass variation, or simply variation. The diagrammatic map below indicates the approximate location of the magnetic North Pole and shows lines of declination that indicate how far east or west of true north a compass will point in a particular area.

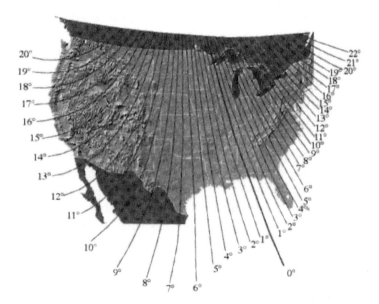

Magnetic declination map of the United States.

The line of zero declination where the magnetic compass will point to true north runs from the tip of the Florida panhandle north-northwest to the western tip of Lake Superior. If you are west of this line, your compass will give a reading that is to the east or right of true north. Since the compass is pointing in a direction with higher bearing number on the 360° circle, this number is considered positive. Conversely, if you are east of this line, your compass reading will be to the west or left of true north, and will be considered negative. An old saying—east is least and west is best—is often used to jog a forgetful memory.

The geographic North Pole is north of the magnetic North Pole. If you are west of the line of zero declination, you must subtract declination from your compass measurement to find true north.

true north bearing = magnetic bearing – magnetic declination

If you were at Cape Hatteras on the North Carolina coast, where declination is about 10°E, or –10, the compass needle will point to the left of true north. If you had magnetic compass bearing of 70° here, the following calculation would be used to find true north:

$$\text{true north} = 70° - (-10°) = 80°$$

Knowing when to add and when to subtract is critical to effective use of a compass. If you do the opposite of what is appropriate for your location, instead of eliminating the error, you double it. A surprisingly large number of people get confused, particularly if they are infrequent compass users. A simple visual exercise can allow you to "rediscover" the correct answer.

1. Find an object with a spherical surface; it need not be a complete sphere.
2. Draw a crude map of the lower 48 about where it should be. It can be very crude; just make sure the Florida panhandle and the tip of Lake Superior (Duluth, Minnesota) are sort of correct.
3. Draw a line from the tip of the Florida panhandle to the tip of Lake Superior and extend it as far north as you can. This is the line of zero declination.
4. Mark the North Pole and come back down the line an inch or two and mark the Magnetic North Pole.
5. Mentally stand in Florida and look up the line. Step to the side of the line that your location is in and point back to the line with the hand closest to it, placing the sphere in that hand.
6. Make the two-finger Cub Scout salute with the other hand, and lower it, pointing to the geographic North Pole—the one farther away—with your longest finger (the bird), and to the magnetic North Pole with the index finger of the same hand. Think of your index finger as the compass needle. To find true north, you must adjust for the angle between the fingers. If you have your left hand up and must move counterclockwise to get from the angle of your index finger to the angle of your middle finger, then you must subtract. If you have your right hand up, the opposite is true.

Do this exercise a few times to get comfortable with the concept and you can dramatically simplify it in your mind.

Many land navigators constantly correct for declination by doing just this sort of calculation every time they take a bearing or orient a map. Others take advantage of a feature built into nicer compasses that allows them to rotate the compass ring building in an offset. Another approach that many find more convenient is to draw an accurate line of magnetic declination across the map, sometimes in several locations if you plan to fold it. To do this, some suggest simply placing the compass directly over the declination diagram that appears on many map borders (collars). This strategy will often produce significant errors. The diagram on the left below indicates 1959 center of sheet declination at a point in southern California of 14° East. Measured with a protractor, the diagram is closer to 8°. The one on the right indicates 1969 center of sheet declination in northern Saskatchewan of 13° 46' East. Measured with a protractor, it is closer to 27°, but it also states, "Use diagram only to obtain numeric values."

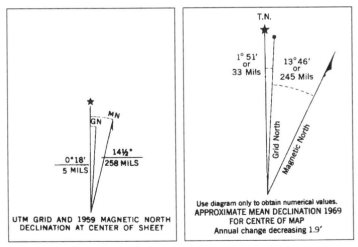

Magnetic Declination diagram from the USGS 7.5 Minute Quad for Earthquake Valley, California, 1959.

Magnetic Declination diagram from the Canada 1:50,000 map for Pelican Narrows, Saskatchewan, 1969.

Web tools are available to calculate past, current, and future magnetic variation for specific locations on earth. The online Compute Values of Earth's Magnetic Field at http://www.ngdc.noaa.gov/seg/geomag/jsp/IGRF.jsp computes the estimated values of the earth's magnetic field, including magnetic declination (D), based on the current International Geomagnetic Reference Field (IGRF). Results are typically accurate to 30' of arc unless short-term solar storms are occurring.

Plugging in the center of map coordinates for the Earthquake Valley quad of 116° 26' 15" W, 33° 3' 15" N and setting a date of January 1, 1959, we get a declination of 14° 33'—for all practical purposes the same as the 14½° on the map collar. Resetting the date for January 1, 2003, we get a declination of 13° 0', a modest difference. What about Pelican Narrows? We could use the same online calculator, or the Canadian Magnetic Information Retrieval Program (MIRP) available online at http://www.geolab.nrcan.gc.ca/geomag/e_cgrf.html#MIRP. For the center of map location of 102°

Pinch the map at the corner and at the portion of the map that represent the degrees of declination. Bite it with your lips. Slide then back and forth and create a crease.

45'W, 55° 7' 30" N, we get a 1969 declination of 16° 26'—rather more than indicated on the map. Checking further, we get a 2003 declination of 10° 22', more than 6° less than the 1969 value from the same source!

So what's the big deal? Is it really necessary to correct for declination? It depends on how far you need to travel,

Using a hard edge, like the back of a small knife blade, firm up the crease marking the line of declination.

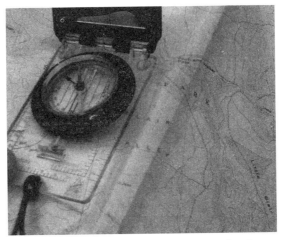

You now have a line (edge) with which to properly orient your map using the compass Magnetic North bearing.

how accurately you need to navigate, and the magnitude of the declination in the area you are in. For every 1° of declination, you will track right (or left) just about 92 feet for every mile you travel. If your next leg is 1.25 miles, your declination is 5° east, and you do not correct, you will arrive about 575 feet (1.25 miles × 5° × 92 feet) left of your intended destination. Even if terrain permitted, few people can walk and hold a course within 5° unless they have a visual marker near or beyond their destination. Unless you are navigating in the dark or in dangerous terrain, a few hundred feet is seldom that big a deal. But as the distance and declination increase, the error increases rapidly. Five miles at a 15° declination will have you more than 1.3 miles off. If you added when you should have subtracted, it will double, and if you are not lost you are certainly not getting where you planned to go.

The well organized will get all the correct maps, check the current declination for each, and, with a flat surface, protractor, and straightedge, draw lines of declination though the center of the map and perhaps at the quarter points across it. Well, some of us just never get quite that organized. The declination value is on the bottom of the map, as is the date, and we know about how much it is changing each year (some maps indicate the annual change value). How can we "draw" a reasonably accurate declination line on the map in the field without a protractor? Each map series requires a different approach.

The standard USGS 7.5' quad has a borderless (also called uncollared) north-south dimension of 22⅝ inches. Each side of the map represents true north. Starting in the lower left-hand corner of the borderless map and proceeding clockwise, label the four corners A, B, C, and D. If you are west of the line of zero declination, start at A. If you are east of the line of zero declination, start at D. The line along the edge of the map must rotate about its bottom end (A or D) inward toward the center of the map, such that when it is extended to intersect the horizontal line that defines the top of the borderless map the distance from the upper corner (B or C) is 0.40 inch for each degree of declination (the tangent of 1° is 0.017455, and 22.625 × 0.17455 = 0.395, rounded to 0.40). If you find yourself without a measuring device, improvise. The graphic scale in the bottom center of the border area has three bars. The middle one is in feet, and the left 1,000-foot section is further divided into 200-foot increments. Each 200-foot bar is approximately 0.10 inch. Using a scrap of paper and some sort of marking instrument (preferably a pencil or pen; if you forgot those too, score it with a knife; if you forgot your knife, go home), mark off multiple 0.40-inch increments; five works well. Go to the top of the sheet and mark off the correct declination. An easy way to mark the declination line on the map is to fold it along the line connecting point A or D and the point where the rotated line intersects the top border. Crease the line firmly so it will retain its shape. Turn the map upside down and repeat the process, creating two parallel lines. Sometimes it is helpful to create a third line by holding the first two together and creasing between them, much like folding a blanket. Finally, fold the map into a smaller rectangle to fit into your map case. Flexible waterproof map cases are available commercially, but we usually use a 2-gallon zipper-lock freezer bag.

How can a magnetic compass be so important if the magnetic field is different everywhere and is steadily changing? Compasses are inexpensive, "self-powered," and work about everywhere except around large metal objects. Nothing else is simpler or more reliable when properly used.

CHAPTER 13

What to Do If You're Really Lost

Unfortunately, the unexpected still happens on occasion while we're outdoors, and we can become lost, even when equipped with our trusty GPS receiver. There are a number of ways in which individuals can become lost. This chapter discusses some of these ways and suggests methods to prevent or overcome them.

DEAD BATTERIES

The Achilles' heel of all GPS receivers is their need for electrical energy. Once the batteries in your GPS receiver are truly dead, it becomes nothing more than a poor-quality rock. If your GPS receiver is plugged into your vehicle's 12-volt electrical adapter, this is not a problem, unless you run out of gas. On the trail, however, a GPS receiver can discharge a set of ordinary batteries in as little as three to four hours. If you are going to rely on your GPS receiver in potentially dangerous or hazardous circumstances, take care to ensure that it will work when you need it—and have an alternative plan in case it doesn't.

It is important to match your power management strategy to your trip plans. If it's a long trip and the GPS is important to your success or safety, turn it off except when essential to check location. This will often mean using a compass or landmarks to maintain course.

One of the biggest sources of battery drain in a GPS receiver is the display screen backlight. If you can avoid using the backlight, you can substantially increase the battery life of your receiver.

Battery Fundamentals

Batteries vary in the amount of energy they store and how much of it they will release based on type, prior use, and environmental conditions. Depleted batteries must either be replaced with backups or recharged. There are a number of different types of batteries available today to power a GPS receiver. Different batteries have many unique features that give them an advantage under certain conditions. Both disposable and rechargeable batteries are available. To get the most out of your GPS receiver, it is important that you select a battery compatible with your planned GPS usage. The rest of this section contains a brief description of some of the various battery types available today and discusses some of the advantages and disadvantages of each type.

Basically, all batteries produce electrical energy from a chemical reaction. The specific chemicals involved in the battery determine the amount of energy it can produce and whether or not it can be recharged. As a general rule, batteries that can be recharged are more expensive than nonrechargeable batteries. Similarly, the price of a battery is more or less directly proportionate to the amount of electrical energy it can produce.

The table opposite summarizes some of the characteristics of the basic types of batteries.

GPS receivers require electrical energy, from either an internal battery or external power connection. Electrical energy in watts is equal to amps times voltage. An older basic GPS unit without mapping capability typically consumes somewhere between 225 and 540 milliwatts. One milliwatt equals 0.001 watt. Most GPS receivers use two or four common 1.5-volt AA batteries. These electrical energy storage devices are typically rated in milliampere-hours (mAh), a measure of how much current they can provide over time. A

SUMMARY OF BATTERY CHARACTERISTICS

BATTERY TYPE	VOLTAGE	GENERAL CHARACTERISTICS	PROS AND CONS
Carbon-zinc	1.5 volts	Most common battery, non-rechargeable, poor storage density, very cheap	Pro: inexpensive Con: low storage density, short life
Alkaline	1.5 volts	Generally non-rechargeable, storage density about twice that of the carbon-zinc cell, but several times more expensive	Pro: longer life than Carbon-Zinc Con: more expensive than Carbon-Zinc
Nickel-cadmium (NiCad)	1.2 volts	The original rechargeable cell for portable gear, now used mostly in gear that needs high power levels on demand	Pro: rechargeable Con: shorter life in GPS receivers than Alkaline batteries
Nickel-metal hydride (NiMH)	1.2 volts	Greater capacity than NiCads but more expensive	Pro: no "memory" problem (do not have to be fully discharged to completely recharge) Con: must be charged before initial use, more expensive than NiCad batteries
Lithium-manganese dioxide	3 volts	The most common nonrechargeable lithium cell	Pro: rechargeable Con: uncommon in GPS receivers
Lithium disulfide	1.5 volts	Voltage-compatible lithium cell as direct replacement for carbon-zinc or alkaline cells	Pro: same voltage as standard AA means direct replacement, work well in colder temperatures Con: expensive
Lithium-iron	3.6 volts	Rechargeable lithium cell	Pro: Performs well under extreme temperatures; holds charge for years Con: Expensive, many not recyclable

rating of 1,000 mAh means that the battery should theoretically be able to supply 1,000 milliamps (mA) for 1 hour, or 100 milliamps for 10 hours, and so on. The most common alkaline cells are rated at around 750 mAh, although you will have to do some digging to learn that because the packages are seldom labeled. High-end NiMH AA cells have ratings of 1,700 to 1,800 mAh. Unfortunately, many users fail to read the fine print and pop them out of the package and into the GPS, only to experience a useful life shorter than ordinary alkalines. To get their full performance they must be recharged right out of the package and before use. Most manufacturers recommend you recharge again if the last recharge was more than a week ago.

Just as your EPA highway mileage doesn't tell the whole story, the mAh rating of a battery is only a test rating. We are interested in how much total energy a battery can deliver under real GPS-use conditions. One problem that makes comparing the performance of two different types of batteries difficult is that even if we buy them new at the store, we have no way of knowing what sort of environments they have been in since they left the factory. For example, new batteries that have been left for some time in a railcar parked on a siding in the northern United States and thus exposed to cold winter temperatures may have a somewhat shorter life than other batteries that were shipped through areas with warmer climates.

Nevertheless, some GPS receiver battery life comparisons have been made. Typically, we would expect between 20 and 24 hours of GPS receiver operation from a set of quality alkaline batteries. Lithium batteries may provide up to 31 hours of operation. Alkaline batteries are generally much cheaper than lithium batteries, although lithium batteries will generally perform better in cold temperatures, which might be a consideration if you're planning on using your GPS unit in cold weather. Lithium batteries also have a longer shelf life.

NiCad batteries in GPS receivers will generally last only five to eight hours, but they can be recharged almost indefinitely. Thus, they may be an economical choice if you have access to a charger or are willing to change out the batteries with a fresh set every few hours.

NiMH batteries offer another option for GPS receiver power. They can run longer than the NiCad batteries and are also rechargeable.

There are also some rechargeable alkaline batteries available. They do not have the life of the regular alkaline batteries, lasting only 10 to 16 hours. They can be recharged about 25 times before their useful life begins to diminish.

Beyond Spare AAs

If you are on an outing that will require continuous GPS use for many hours or you really want to lug that PDA along, despite its relatively short battery life, some useful equipment is available. The Pocket Power Pak marketed by Beacon 5 (http://www.beacon5.com) contains three D cells with a total rated capacity of 18,000 mAh. With batteries, it adds 22 ounces to your pack. Models are available for a wide variety of PDAs and can increase run time up to 20-fold.

Another interesting option is the zinc air chargers for portable electronics marketed by Instant Power (http://www.instant-power.com/). These units consist of a charger module with control circuitry, a custom cord connecting the charger to the electronic device, and disposable zinc-air batteries. Batteries for PDAs are typically 2 by 2.7 by 0.5 inches, weigh 76 grams (2.7 ounces), and provide up to three recharges. The batteries must be stored in an airtight bag between charges.

Battery Chargers

Rechargeable batteries offer the best value over time, but getting the most energy—and thereby run time—from an individual charge requires proper selection and use of the charging device. Studies show that improper charging can reduce energy stored by a factor of two. Chargers that use a combination of early fast charge and later-phase trickle charge seem to yield the most stored energy and longest battery life.

With rechargeable batteries in your GPS receiver, you have several recharging options. Battery chargers that work directly off the common 120-volt AC system are widely available. These are useful if you are near a facility that has standard electrical service: You can simply plug the charger into a standard convenience outlet and insert the batteries in the charger.

Some chargers also work off the standard 12-volt DC electrical systems used in cars and trucks. In this case you can plug the charger into the vehicle's cigarette lighter socket or other auxiliary 12-volt outlet and recharge your GPS receiver batteries from a vehicle. This is a convenient option if you are operating in a situation where you frequently return to your vehicle.

In more remote situations, there are chargers that work directly from photovoltaic cells. These devices produce DC-charging current from direct sunlight. Such charging units are more expensive and, of course, have to be placed in direct sunlight to work; still, they can be used to recharge batteries in very remote locations. Since the output of photovoltaic chargers is limited, the time required to fully recharge batteries will generally be longer. These units tend to be large and somewhat heavy. They are probably best suited for a base-camp-style operation as they would be difficult to carry while hiking.

There are also small portable hand-crank generators available. These generators produce electrical power when the human operator rotates a hand crank attached to the generator shaft. While these devices can be used to recharge batteries, they are more commonly used to provide temporary power to the GPS receiver, since it would take an extended period of cranking to recharge the batteries.

YOUR GPS IS DEAD, YOU LOST THE COMPASS, AND YOU NEED TO FIND DIRECTION

This is a guide to GPS, not an outdoor survival manual. Many useful outdoor survival guides are available; just go to Amazon.com on the Web and search for "outdoor survival." There are also quite a number of useful Web sites focusing on outdoor survival, and a useful directory is available at http://www. wilderness-survival.net/topsites/index.php. One of the most widely used guides to outdoor survival is the U.S. Army Survival Manual, FM21-76. New, it sells for around $15, but used copies in good condition can be found on the Web or at used-book stores for as little as $5. If your outdoor journeys take you to remote places, you should own and study this book.

Finding Direction

There are many basic ways to get yourself oriented, permitting you to travel consistently in the general direction you want to go. None of these will have the accuracy of a GPS receiver or a decent compass, but they will keep you from heading in the wrong direction or walking in circles. Once you are confident you have oriented yourself, it is important to regularly update your direction of travel. If you can pick a distant natural feature like a peak or a human-made feature like a tower light, use it as a destination marker to help maintain track. Better yet, identify two distant landmarks, one significantly farther away than (behind) the other. You can walk around a single landmark, but keeping two aligned—sometimes called "riding the range"—will keep you on a tight course.

The Shadow Tip Method

Regardless of where you are on the planet, the sun rises in the east and sets in the west. The following method for finding direction is cited in many survival methods, but has its limitations. First, here's a quick version for use on the move:

- Find a reasonably straight stick about a yard in length.
- Find an area where the sun's shadow is unobstructed, and the ground reasonably flat. Drive the stick into the ground.
- Using a pebble, a stick, or any handy small object, mark the tip of the shadow cast by the stick.
- Wait 10 to 20 minutes and the shadow will have moved 1.5 to 2 inches. Mark the end of the shadow again.
- Draw a line from the first mark to the second, and continue the line for another foot.
- Place your left foot at the first mark and your right foot at the other end of the line. In the northern temperate zone, you will be looking in a northerly direction; if you are in the southern temperate zone, you will be looking in a southerly direction.

Use a shorter stick in winter and a piece of paper, unless on sand or dirt. This method works much better in the middle of the day.

Mark the shadow tip with a pebble, stick, or mark on paper. This example in the midafternoon winter shows the method has its limitations.

This longer method for use in camp is more accurate:

➤ Have the stick in place and be up for sunrise. Mark the tip of the shadow just as the sun is fully above the horizon.

➤ Using a string and a stick, strike an arc with the base of the stick as the center and the radius equal to the length of the shadow, extending it to the other side of the stick. At sunset, mark the point where the shadow hits the arc.

➤ The line between the two points connects west and east.

Using a Watch as a Crude Compass

You can use a watch to determine direction in the temperate zones (23.4° to 66.6' north or south latitude). The method varies depending on which hemisphere you are in. It's easier with a conventional analog watch, but with a bit of improvising a digital watch will suffice.

Cast a shadow across the hour hand. South is midway between the shadow and noon. Look carefully and you can see that the compass needle agrees.

➤ Place a small, straight stick in the ground in a level, unobstructed location.

➤ In the northern temperate zone, place the watch on the ground so that the hour (short) hand aligns with the shadow cast by the stick.

➤ In the southern temperate zone, place the watch on the ground so that the imaginary line passing through the center of the watch and 12 o'clock aligns with the shadow cast by the stick.

➤ Draw an imaginary line across the face of the watch, passing midway between 12 o'clock and the hour hand. This imaginary line defines north and south.

- If your watch is set to Daylight Saving Time, set the line midway between one o'clock and the hour hand.
- If you have a digital watch, draw a round analog watch face on a small piece of paper, placing the hour hand where the digital watch indicates. If you don't have paper, scratch it on the ground.
- If you must hurry, skip the stick and just point the hour hand at the sun.

Basic Celestial Direction Finding

All other stars revolve around Polaris, the North Star or Pole Star. When you find it, you are looking true north.

The North Star is part of the constellation Ursa Minor, or the Little Dipper. It is the last star in the handle.

The easiest way to find north is to first find the larger constellation Ursa Major, or the Big Dipper. A line drawn from the bottom star of the Dipper opposite the handle and through the star above on the rim of the Dipper points to the North Star. The North Star is about five times the distance from the "rim" as the distance between the two pointing stars.

On the opposite side of the North Star, about equidistant from the Big Dipper, is the constellation Cassiopeia. It is dominated by five stars that form a squashed M or W pattern. The North Star lies straight out from the center star of Cassiopeia.

The Moon

If the moon rises before the sun has set, the illuminated side will be on the west. If the moon rises after midnight, the illuminated side will be in the east.

Natural Indicators

If you travel in the same region a fair amount and are observant, over time you can accumulate knowledge that will help you determine direction.

Across much of the Great Plains, the dominant wind direction is from the south. The few trees you encounter are often "flagged," with their upper branches bent, clearly pointing north.

The wide leaves of perennial prairie plant *Silphium laciniatum*, commonly known as the compass plant, polar plant, or even turpentine plant, usually align themselves north-south. The plant can be identified by its very flat, lobed, hairy lower leaves and late-summer bright yellow flowers. While 3-foot-high plants are common, it can reach 12 feet. It's part of the rosin-weed family; you can distinguish it from the sunflower by breaking the stem to check for sap. Native Americans reported used the sap as a chewing gum.

Snow will melt first on the south side of objects, and moisture will remain longest on the north side.

Making a Simple Compass

If you have a small piece of ferrous metal, you can make a primitive compass. Needles or fine wire work well, as does part of a razor blade. Magnetize the metal by slowly and repeatedly passing it through a piece of silk fabric, always in the same direction. Lacking silk, use your hair. If you are bald-well, look elsewhere. If you have a battery of at least 2 volts (or can string a couple together in series) and some wire, you can magnetize the metal electrically. Make a wire coil and connect the ends to the battery. Repeatedly pass the object to be magnetized in and out of the coil (if the wire is not insulated, wrap the object in paper).

Suspend the magnetized object from a nonmetallic string or thread. Use hair or plant fiber if you don't have string. An alternative is to float the object on a piece of paper or a small piece of wood in water. The object will align itself north-south.

APPENDIX A

Bibliography

Hjellstrom, Bjorn, *Be Expert with Map and Compass*, John Wiley & Sons, 1994.

U.S. Department of Defense, *U.S. Army Survival Manual FM 21-76*.

Useful Web Sites

The ever-evolving World Wide Web provides a vast treasure trove of GPS, map, and land navigation information. Some sites were noted in the text; other interesting sites are listed below. For additional information on a specific topic, use a good search engine like Google. It's amazing how much information you can find on the Web with a bit of digging.

GPS Manufacturers

http://www.garmin.com/
http://www.lowrance.com/
http://www.delorme.com/
http://leadtek.com/
http://www.maptech.com/products/PocketNavigator/
    index.cfm

GPS Sales and Reviews

http://www.thegpsstore.com
http://www.gps4fun.com

Maps and Mapmaking

http://www.esri.com/software/arcpad/index.html
http://www.delorme.com/
http://www.fugawi.com
http://www.cgrer.uiowa.edu/servers/servers
    _references.html

Magazines
http://www.gpsworld.com/

Geocaching
http://www.geocaching.com/

Useful Sites
http://www.windows.ucar.edu/tour/link=/earth/
    statistics.html
http://www.colorado.edu/geography/gcraft/notes/gps/
    gps.html
http://www.instant-power.com/sales/online_sales.shtml
http://www.teletype.com/pages/gps/compatibility.html
http://www.unc.edu/~rowlett/units/index.html
http://www.tapr.org/~kh2z/Waypoint/

 **Index**

Rotational axis, 39
Routes, 21, 23; planning,
    88

Satellites, 9, 13–14, 84
Scales, 49, 124
Selective Availability, 17
Shadow Tip Method, 179
SmartMap, IMS, 106
Software, Programs, 89,
    90; GARtrip, 90;
    EasyGPS, 91;
    TopoGrafix, 91;
    TerraServer, 91;
    Pharos, 111; TeleType
    GPS, 111; Delorme,
    114; Street Atlas USA
    2008, 115
SPCS, 45
Stadium, 146

State Plane Coordinate
    System (SPCS), 45
Synchronization, 12

Time, measuring, 11
Tracks, 21, 23, 87
Triangulation, 10

U.S. Army Survival
    Manual, 179
U.S. Forest Service, 139
U.S. Geological Survey,
    113, 131, 132
Universal Transverse
    Mercator (UTM), 42

WAAS, 16
Waypoints, 21, 22, 87
Wide Area Augmentation
    System (WAAS), 16